"A Comprehensive Guide for Coaches who Coach Kids How to Ski"

The sign of greater educational writings is not always indicated by the immediate value they lend to targeted and specific audiences. "A Comprehensive Guide for Coaches Who Coach Kids How to Ski" , while meant for Alpine ski coaches and instructors, provides key information for Snow Sports resort management and perhaps beyond. The wring of "A Comprehensive Guide for Coaches Who Coach Kids How to Ski" has also provided vetted outlines in regard to the 2021 pandemic landscape that finds children's participation outdoor activities on the rise. The author wrote this book with a lot of passion.

Brad Miller
Director, Nub's Nob Winter Sports School
PSIA-AASI-C, Nordic and Children's Educational Staff
PSIA Alpine, Level 3
PSIA Cross Country, Level 3
PSIA Telemark, Level 3
PSIA Children's Specialist 2
PSIA Free Style Specialist 1

- -

'A Comprehensive Guide for Coaches Who Coach Kids How to Ski' is an easy read that offers really useful and thought-provoking techniques that can help elevate the craft of any ski coach that works with children. It explores numerous facets of the rewarding, yet challenging world of children's snow sports instruction and helps coaches expand their knowledge base so they can be more effective on the hill.

Greg Chmielecki
Alpine Administrator-PSIA-Central Division Education Staff
Director, Vail Resorts Educational Staff
PSIA Alpine, Level 3

This book provides the reader with a 'one-stop shop' for information on the 'Art and Science' of teaching snow sports to children. The author provides unique insights into the 'What, How, and Why' of a child's physical and mental learning process; how a snow sports instructor should approach the lesson with a child, from building a relationship with both the child and parent, by accessing the child's Student Profile and the organization of an appropriate lesson. Also, the author provides many tips for the parent to ensure that their child will get the most out of the lesson. This book is a must for any coach or ski instructor involved in teaching snow sports to children.

Jon Stepleton
Former Director of Children's Advanced Teaching Specialist (Vail Resorts at Boston Mills, Brandywine, & Alpine Valley Ski Resorts)
PSIA Alpine, Level 3
PSIA Telemark, Level 3
PSIA Children's Specialist 2
PSIA Instructor for 30 years

This is a stellar effort, which nails it, in an effort to cover all aspects of effectively and efficiently coaching children to ski. A fabulous resource in so many ways. No other children's book is available in one comprehensive source as this book.

Mike Kaltenstein
PSIA Alpine, Level 3, PSIA Children's Specialist, Level 1
PSIA Senior Specialist, Level 1; Vail Resorts Educational Staff
PSIA Alpine Trainer

A Comprehensive Guide
For Coaching Children
How To Ski

A Quick Guide to:

- How to become an outstanding kid's coach
- How to Bond with the parent and child
- Organizing bulletproof lesson plans
- Building safety into your coaching
- Using proper ski tools, props, games for successful lessons
- Dealing with special behaviors and challenges
- Teaching different age groups with more fun
- Coaching beginner to advanced lessons
- Discovering solutions for difficult students
- How to inspire children's minds to learn quicker
- Learning how to exceed customer's satisfaction 100 percent of the time

Herbert K. Naito

To order additional copies of this book, contact:
Proisle Publishing Services LLC
1177 6th Ave 5th Floor
New York, NY 10036, USA
Phone: (+1 347-922-3779)
info@proislepublishing.com

PROISLE PUBLISHING

TABLE OF CONTENTS

SOMETHING ABOUT THE AUTHOR

He spent 40 years in the medical profession. For fun, he coached skiing for over 20 years. He is a member of the Professional Ski Instructors of America, and is certified in Alpine Skiing, Level 2; Adaptive Specialist, Level 1; Children's Specialist, Level 2; PSIA Senior Specialist, Level 2; and Children's Trainer. Currently he is employed by the Vail Ski Resorts and is presently on the Vail Educational Staff. He was the former Director of the Children's Advanced Training Specialist, and the Express Pre-School School Ski Programs.

In addition to this book, he has written seven other books on skiing:

(1) How to Prepare for your Child's First Ski Lesson,

(2) The Funky Donkey Tells His Story About His First Ski Lesson,

(3) Coaching Wacky Racoon, Children, and Adults the Fundamentals of Good Sportsmanship,

(4) The Hidden Secrets of Having Fun At and Around the Ski Resorts,

(5) How to Create Fun for Children with Disabilities on the Ski Slopes,

(6) How to Create a Successful Ski Lesson for Senior Citizens,

(7) How God Prepared & Inspired Me to be a Writer and Author,

INTRODUCTION

Every ski resort has focused on developing children's programs. This handbook is intended to assist Alpine Ski Instructors to be more effective and efficient when coaching kids how to ski. Teaching kids is an ART, a SKILL, and a PASSION. The goal is to present clear, concise, and validated methods to teach the proper movements to get the skis to turn down different types of terrain in a precise, effective and controlled manner. Much of my knowledge comes from methods, techniques, and concepts learned from the Professional Ski Instructors of America (PSIA), years of experimenting with what really works with kids, and collecting and validating thoughts of our PSIA ski instructors at Boston Mills (BM), Brandywine (BW), and Alpine Valley (AV) Ski Resorts in Ohio (now owned and operated by *Vail Resorts Management Group*.

In 2006, the BM/BW Director, Mike Bell, commissioned Jon Stepelton to create a Children's Training Program for BM and BW Ski Resorts. Jon accepted the Directorship of the new Children's Advanced Training Staff (CATS) and formed his committee members with Joe Huber, Annette Lang, Leigh Owen, Jen Nobel, Marilyn Yonek, and John Gomersal. Their task was to develop the training format and materials for what became the Accredited Children's Advanced Training Specialist Program. The objective was to create an in-house instructor-training program to enhance their teaching skills at both BM/BW; this provided a unified and standardized approach for its children's programs. This training program gave the instructors the building blocks to craft unforgettable memories for their students and parents. This program established consistency in teaching children throughout all of the different programs, regardless of age. When the instructors completed the classroom and on-snow portions of training, they were awarded with the "Gold" Certified Children's Instructor Logo.

Jon passed the directorship to me in 2012. I have expanded the BM/BW CATS Accredited program to include Alpine Valley Ski Resorts. All three resorts are under one CATS directorship. I have been coaching skiing for over 20 years and one of my unique accomplishments was the development of a one-of-a-kind Express Preschool Ski School, whereby we train the kids' *parents* how to coach their three- to four-year-old tikes how to ski and have fun on the slopes. This program was created to reduce the separation anxiety between parent and child and to help create a bonding relationship between the two, with lasting fun and memories on the snow. The parents were taught the fundamentals of proper movements to get the skis to turn and to help guide their children's experiences on the snow. This program had an edge over a conventional kid's program because it had the economic advantage of having one children's specialist coach for three to five kids and their parents. The baton was passed to the third CATS Director, Koren Griffis (aka Coco), in 2020.

It should be noted that Sonja Rom and Sandy Kirshner, were former co-directors of the *'Mogul Mites' Program* (Five-to seven-year-old) at BM and BW Ski Resorts. They realized the need for training instructors in the art and science of teaching kids; so, they created the Children's Accreditation program at PSIA-Central Division. Then they became the first clinicians and examiners for the program. In recent years, this program has evolved into the popular Children's Specialist 1 and 2 Certification programs offered by PSIA-National.

This book is filled with tips on ski props, fun games, tricks, and tactics that can enhance the learning performance of children on the snow. Every effort has been made to inject everyday practical tips and experiences that can be helpful to you as Snow Sport instructors to make your coaching more engaging, fun, and rewarding for the kids. The backbone of this handbook is the fundamental methods and teaching techniques of PSIA.

The objective of this handbook is to (1) consolidate the scattered *golden nuggets* of information found in the many books, manuals, magazines, handouts in clinics, PSIA and other online videos, PSIA e-courses, (2) to collect and share the *creative* coaching with unique a-ha moments observed over the years that have illuminated the kids' lightbulbs, letting them grasp complex concepts, and (3) explain special circumstances (The problematic child, slow learners, and children with special needs). These priceless gems should help instructors with the learning curve so they become better teachers.

This document is geared toward teaching kids, but it can serve as a template and can be expanded to coach adults and teach other PSIA disciplines, such as Adaptive Skiing, Telemark Skiing, Snowboarding, Freestyle, Cross-Country Skiing, and Senior Specialist Skiing. This is not a standalone manual but should be used in conjunction with other PSIA technical manuals. I made every attempt to personalize this book to add realistic concepts so these issues and concepts work in everyday life. Real-life stories and comments were added because the experiences have been time tested. I am certain many of you have your own experiences that have produced memorable a-ha moments. In addition, I have added real-life photographs at key locations in the text to clarify the topics being covered, acknowledging that a picture is worth a thousand words. Many of the common words used in skiing have been modified because of copyright restrictions (e.g., People-mover conveyer belt, plastic hoop, flying disc, ski harnesses, ski-tip connector).

Finally, I want to thank my colleagues, PSIA, and friends in helping me assemble this handbook.

This published book was supported by a generous grant from the Dr. and Mrs. Herbert K. Naito Charitable Foundation.

Pineapple Herb

ACKNOWLEDGMENTS

I would like to extend my humble gratitude to the entire Editorial Board. Without their invaluable expertise, their knowledge, skills and experiences, I would not have been able to compose this handbook. The graphic artist and professional photographer also did an outstanding job in bringing this book together.

Review Board:

Robert Abbott: PSIA Alpine, Level 3; PSIA Trainer; PSIA Alpine Examiner; Vail Resorts Ed Staff

Paul Antczak: PSIA Alpine, Level 1; PSIA Children's Specialist, Level 1

Greg Chimeleki: PSIA Alpine, Level 3; PSIA Children's Specialist, Level 2; PSIA Trainer: PSIA-C, Examiner; PSIA Free Style, Level 1; PSIA-C Examiner; Vail Resorts Ed Staff

Mikel Kaltenstein: PSIA Alpine, Level 3; PSIA Children's Specialist, Level 1; PSIA Senior Specialist, Level 1; PSIA Children's Trainer; Vail Resorts Ed Staff

Koren Griffis: PSIA Alpine, Level 2; PSIA Children's Specialist, Level 2; PSIA Senior Specialist: PSIA Children's Trainer; Vail Resorts Ed Staff

Carlton Guc: PSIA Alpine, Level 3; PSIA Children's Specialist, Level 1; PSIA Senior Specialist, Level 1; PSIA-C, Education Staff; Vail Resorts Ed Staff.

Phillip Howell: ASSI Snowboard, Level 3; PSIA Trainer; ASSI and PSIA Examiner; PSIA-C Ed Staff, Children's Specialist and Cross Country; Vail Resorts Ed Staff

Joseph Huber: PSIA Alpine, Level 2; PSIA Adaptive, Level 2, PSIA Telemark, Level 1, PSIA Children's Specialist, Level 2; PSIA Senior Specialist, Level I; PSIIA Adaptive Trainer; PSIA Trainer; Vail Resorts Ed Staff

John Lang: PSIA Alpine, Level 3; PSIA Children's Specialist, Level 1; PSIA Telemark, Level 1; Veil Resorts Ed Staff.

Rebecca Madick: PSIA Alpine, Level 3; PSIA Children's Specialist, Level 2; PSIA Senior Specialist

Robert Madick: PSIA Alpine, Level 2; PSIA C
children's Specialist, Level 2

Bradfred Miller: PSIA Alpine, Level 3; PSIA Children's Specialist, Level 2; PSIA Trainer; PSIA Telemark, Level 3; PSIA Cross Country, Level 3, PSIA-C Nordic Education Staff

Jon Stepelton: PSIA Alpine, Level 3; PSIA Children's Specialist, Level 2; PSIA Telemark, Level 3; PSIA Trainer; Vail Resorts Ed Staff

Sonja Rom: PSIA Alpine, Level 3; PSIA Alpine Trainer; PSIA Children's Trainer; PSIA Alpine Examiner

Marilyn Yonek: PSIA Alpine, Level 3; PSIA Trainer; Children's Specialist Level 2; Vail Resorts Ed Staff

Professional Photographer:

Jennifer Barnwell: PSIA Alpine, Level I; PSIA Children's Specialist, Level 1

Graphic Artist:

Jon Stepelton: PSIA Alpine, Level 3; PSIA Children's Specialist, Level 2;PSIA Telemark, Level 3; PSIA Children's Specialist, Level 2 and Alpine, Level 3 Trainer; Vail Resorts Ed Staff

CHAPTER 1

Developing a Strong Foundation—Building a Relationship between the Parent and the Child

I cannot overemphasize how critical it is for *you*, the coach, to establish a *bond* and *trust*[16] with both the *parent* and their child. The learning connection with children requires all three of you to be successful through the bonding process. My first clue on the importance of bonding and trust came when I got a new animal to respond to my command. Have you ever noticed that when you get a new pet (Or even a newborn baby), they seldom gravitate to you immediately? You need to spend quality time to bond and develop trust with the cat, dog, horse, rabbit, or baby; otherwise, it won't happen! Over the years, I had four equine students that had a deep passion for horse riding that wanted to learn skiing. I curiously communicated with them and did a lot of research on horse training[35, 45, 51]. You know, there are a lot of similarities with training people how to ski and training them how to ride a horse.

For example,

1. You cannot ride a horse before developing a relationship; bonding and developing trust with one another is crucial. Likewise, a ski instructor that does not bond and develop trust with a ski student, will have difficulties with executing his/her ski lessons.

2. The bonding needs to be reinforced frequently by verbal communications, with body gestures (Rubbing the nose, forehead, neck areas called a "horse handshake"), and rewards; likewise, kids need the same treatment by their coaches to maintain the bonding process.

3. Safety is first; wearing a helmet is primary along with a properly fitted riding boots.

4. Going slow before you ride faster (Walk, trot, canter, gallop) is always suggested; likewise, skiing on safe and gentle terrain and slowly is required before going fast, and even racing.

5. Learning to ride in a balanced position in the saddle is required before learning other fundamental movements; likewise, in skiing, we want the student to master balance throughout the turns on the hills of different steepness.

6. The rider is required to be in synchronization and alignment with the galloping horse's rhythm; just as a skier's core (Center of Mass) needs to be in alignment with his/her feet (Base of Support).

7. A horse does not want to be treated roughly or be too tightly controlled; neither does a student.

I tell you this tidbit of information because it can make you a better ski coach. How?

By being creative; your job is to develop a lesson plan that will unlock your students' interests, motivation, and excitement about wanting to learn everything about skiing. To find the key to the lock, you need to discover where the key is located by asking a lot of creative questions, like what kind of sports, movies, or hobbies do you have a passion for?

If I find *horse lovers* in the class, I always develop a lesson plan around *horse-riding training* because the learning curve is faster for those students. Sometimes, you may not have the time to connect with the parent and child because of special circumstances, for example, when the classes consist of six or more students. However, you should adapt these concepts to group lessons whenever circumstances allow it. This manual primarily relates to private lessons. I'll start with the multiple ways that you can bond and develop trust with your students:

A. Before the On-Snow Lesson:

Assure the parent (And child, for that matter) that *safety*[16] is your highest priority; you will protect their child as if they were your very own.

Make *fun* is your second-highest priority. You will make every effort to make their lessons *fun* and memorable.

Don't forget to incorporate Maslow's Hierarchy of Needs drawing[13, 16, 31, 50] (See figure 1) in your lesson plans (e.g., Has the child eaten any food recently, taken any liquid for proper hydration? Did they go to the bathroom just before the lesson? Have they taken their needed medications? Are they properly dressed for the outside temperature and wind? Do they have safety gear? Maslow's Hierarchy of Needs is a personality, learning, and motivational theory in psychology comprising a five-tier model of human needs describing what drives and motivates people. Needs lower down in the pyramid must be satisfied before individuals can attain the needs higher up. Self-actualization is the full realization of one's creative, intellectual, and social potential through internal drive. It's leveraging one's abilities to reach their potential.

Figure 1. This modified Maslow's Hierarchy of Needs was adapted for kids[12, 16, 31, 50]

During your introduction, share with them your background, hobbies, and other interests (e.g., What you do when you are not at the ski school, what pets you own, what kind of work you do). How many instructors do you know that just introduce themselves as follows?, "Hi, my name is Joe, I'm your coach for today." Which of the two approaches is more likely to create bonding?

Ask the parent if they want a picture of their child as they take the lesson to preserve the memory.

When talking to your client, formulate a student profile. Ask, "What sports they like to participate in? What fun activities do you like to do? What TV shows do you like to watch? What pets do you own? Where do you go on your summer vacations?" Make every attempt to befriend them and know who they are, what motivates them, and what they like and dislike.

Inform both the parent and the child about your commitment to practice safety, will introduce fun, and create innovative learning experiences in the lesson plans at all times.

Practice proper grooming. Show up refreshed, with a clean uniform, speaking slowly, clearly, and deliberately, and with a beautiful, friendly smile. Psychological studies show that a person develops a liking or disliking for a person within the first fifty milliseconds to less than seven seconds.

Always smile. Be as gentle, kind, and caring as you would with your own child. The quality of your nonverbal communication is critical for a secure attachment bond. Smiling makes you more approachable. Studies show that smiles, laughter, and humor all contribute to being more likeable. Swiss researchers found that the stronger the smile, the more attractive a face looked. So, turn on your happy face and add lots of humor to your personality. In this era of the airborne pandemic and the new safety rules[46], the face mask might hinder your exhibition for enthusiasm, happiness, and excitement, so use more body language to communicate (An in-depth discussion on safety with the pandemic will be found in chapter 4).

Make quality time and trust a priority ("Rome wasn't built in a day.") Building Trust[16] with a kid is a priority and will take lots of work. Reinforcing the many acts of love and kindness is key. Kids form their view of themselves and the world around them every day. They need your encouragement to see themselves as good people, capable of doing good things, and they need to know that you are on their side.

Many school programs for the little ones have theme days, (e.g., Pirates Day, Aloha Day, Animal Day, Circus Day, Goofy Day). Dress the part and wear outrageous outfit to connect with the kids and have fun.

Be mindful that *safety* is your highest priority in your lessons. To increase your success with the child, take a first run to examine the snow texture (Powder, ice cookies) and develop a strategy on overcoming some of these difficulties.

B. On-snow Lesson:

Stand tall and speak slowly and clearly to show confidence.

Be a leader and mentor; provide outstanding coaching and be their moral compass both on and off the hill.

Be a cavalier and use appropriate languages and behavior on and off the slopes at all times to affect their mode of thinking and conduct. Be a good listener and respond to all their needs. Become loyal friends on and off the slopes.

Show your enthusiasm - hollering, clapping your hands, jumping around, singing. Would you take a clinic from a staff member who talked in an emotionless and monotone voice or from a funny, exuberant person with lots of energy and extraordinary excitement?

Make having *fun* is your second highest priority, after safety (See figure 2). How will you will make every effort to make their lessons fun-filled and memorable?

Figure 2. Snow Sport motto: Safety, Fun, learning[16]

Understand the PSIA CAP Model (Cognitive, Affective, Physical Developments), [3-5, 13, 33, 46, 47] and know how to use it when assessing the child for developing a customized lesson (See figure 3) Also, see Chapters 8 and 9 for use of this great model.

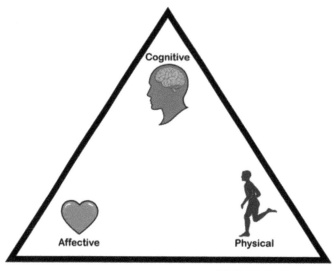

Figure 3. PSIA CAP Model. [3-5, 13, 33, 46, 47]

Be mindful when designing your lesson plan to assess what type of learner they are to accelerate the learning curve.

Be sure the established goals are realistic and not idealistic. Also, separate the parent's goals from the child's goals. More on what the parents can expect for each age groups can be found in chapter 7. The challenges that you can encounter can be found in chapters 2, 3 and 8 and what you can expect in chapter 7.

When communicating with the child, get down on your knees and look them in the eye. How often have you observed a 6'0" instructor standing up to a 2'5" child when giving instructions or just communicating with them with *no eye contact?* The child is just seeing two knee-caps! Is there any possible *bonding* and *trust*[16] taking place? So, as a reminder, try not to wear sunglasses when you are teaching a lesson. If you absolutely must wear goggles that day, try to use a pair with clear lenses. When making eye contact with the parent, introduce yourself, explain your background and experience with coaching kids, and define what your goals are for the day. By all means, do ask them their expectations. Remember, the <u>parent</u> is the customer, and the child is the consumer. Ask the parent if there is any special information that you should know about their precious child (e.g., Autism, diabetes, ADD, ADHD, or any other unique needs or concerns). For example, what are the child's interests, sports participation, favorite school subjects and hobbies, and so on? I cannot overemphasize the importance of communicating on your knees with little children. I have done it so often that every three years; I need to replace my black trousers because I have white spots on each knee. Later, I got wise and purchased sports knee guards!

Photo 1: A coach on her knees and making eye contact to effectively communicate with her student'

You need to be clear, open, and honest to create bonding and trust. For example, tell the parent and child that falling will eventually take place, but do not fret about how many times the child fell; rather, emphasize how the child will learn to get up by themselves. One needs to be careful to not create fear[16] in the child, especially when they are new to the snow sport; instead teach them to fall to the side and learn to get up. Prevent falling back (Behind the ski bindings) as much as possible because of the possibilities of blowing out a knee ligament. Do inform them that falling is fun in the soft snow and when going to a slow speed. Ensure the student that you will teach them the many ways of getting up safely. You can start by practicing falling down in the soft snow without the equipment.

When the child has a meltdown, regroup, stay close, and be compassionate. Find alternate solutions with empathy. Keep your sense of humor and composure at all times. Have patience, and keep working on ways to bond and form a *trust*[16] with the student.

Figure 4: A young boy that did not bond with the coach and is pouting'

Use appropriate *restroom* procedures. A staff member of the same gender must always accompany children to the restroom; they should never go in alone for fear of getting lost or being abducted. A child should never be alone with one adult in the restroom stall. If the child needs help in the stall to assist taking off the layers of clothing, two staff members must accompany the child. If you are out skiing with a group of kids, you should take the entire class with you or ask another staff member (The same gender as the child) if he/she is available to take the student to the restroom.

Demonstrate lots of unconditional, tender, faithful love, and kindness. Most kids are very sensitive, intuitive, and astute when it comes to receiving (Or not receiving) love and kindness. In *"The 5 Love Languages,"* writer Gary Chapman states that there are five primary ways of expressing love and that each of us tends to gravitate toward one of those five forms: (1) words of affirmation, (2) acts of service, (3) receiving gifts, (4) quality time, and (5) physical interactions (high-fives, fist bumps, pole taps). In the past, hugs and hugging were great ways to reward your students, however the new norm for COVID-19 pandemic is to avoid such bodily contact until further notice. I am sure you can come up with multiple of ways in each category to enhance your connection with your students. Try to employ as many different ways to confirm this and by demonstrating genuine love for them when you're coaching and delivering what they want and need. Make this a high-priority routine when you teach kids in all of your lessons. Don't forget to spread this to both the customer and consumer. Show ever-lasting kindness, caring, compassion, and loving ways to help bond the child and parents with you.

Read ski cartoon books to kids.[9, 15, 19, 22, 30, 32, 41, 49] Many ski programs have a time-out Period for rest, snacks, hot chocolate, and the lavatory. During this time, maybe you could read children's ski books (e.g., Squirrels on Skis; The Adventure Friends: Ski Day) to entertain them. You can recommend to the parents that, they too, could read animated cartoon books on skiing (See references) to help motivate their child at home.

Photo 2. After the hot-chocolate time and coloring-book session, a coach reads a cartoon book to children to entertain and help motivate them to ski.

Create fun times with foot drills. Many schools have cut-out feet to illustrate foot movements (e.g., Pizza of different sizes, French fries) as they follow a trail of foot activities. Kicking the ball (i.e.,While standing or sitting down) to the next child in a circle helps with foot dexterity. Walking like a duck and quacking like a duck adds to the fun while learning the herringbone walk up a gentle slope (Walking like a duck) adds rotary skill. Climbing up a small wooden ramp sideways assists with lateral movements and learning to climb the hill in a side step.

Photo 3. Children are doing foot drills indoors to learn various skills.

C. Closing the Lesson:

Confirm the precise time and location where you'll meet the parent after the lesson. Nothing creates more anxiety than when the parent has lost a child or when the child has a lost parent. It is also important that you deliver them on time, as agreed. Failing to do so could ruin your efforts to create a great lesson.

When providing a closure, be sure to explain why, what, how, and where, you taught the lesson. Include the child's many successes on the hill. Never provide a negative comment on what their child did or did not do. Always give positive comments. Make the positive comments first. Regarding any deficiencies, you can say, "On the next lesson, we will be working on so-and-so to enhance the child's skills." Remember, you need always to protect the self-esteem of your students. It is paramount they feel good about themselves and what they are trying to accomplish. Tune in to the parent's feedback; if they appear disappointed with their child's performance, assure them why the child is having difficulty. For example, the child had difficulties turning, inform them that depending on the age of their child

(Usually six years and under), their fine-tuning muscles in their feet and ankles may not be fully developed. The "twisting" motion may be more a "whole-body" movement to get their feet to twist. Inform the parent that at these ages, it is acceptable. But, end with a solution; (i.e., How you are going to improve their performances with their next lesson). Remember the following three things on your feedback:[16] (1) always be nonjudgmental, (2) be certain your comments are always positive and inspirational, (3) besides their child, be sure to inform the parent about the child's performance evaluation.

Whenever you say something to kids, be genuine, transparent, and affirm your conviction that you want to be their close friend. Always be positive and gentle with your comments. Research has shown that it takes five positive comments to help negate the negative a single negative comment you made. So, don't raise your voice or yell at the kid, saying things like, "I said, turning that way to stop is *not* right!" Instead, try saying, "Turning as you did was OK, but let's try another way that is more effective in bringing you to a stop."

Many resorts have shout-out programs, with the goal of recognizing the outstanding deeds a coach did for their child, the parent, or other guests. These accolades will motivate the coach and other instructors to follow the Business Model. For the children's accomplishments, you can give homemade blue ribbons or stickers to your students for their outstanding accomplishments. If your establishment does not have an accolade or shout-out program, create your own by telling your colleagues and management staff how wonderful of a job that they have done; maybe it will catch on and others will join in. Everyone wants to be appreciated! This also motivates the coaches to set higher goals and be more driven in their profession.

Chart the progress of your students. Many schools have their own report-card systems to track kids' knowledge and skills. You can develop your own quick checklist of skills learned, safety, and other accomplishments to review with parents. I have my own log sheets in my portfolio (And a small notebook that fits into my pocket) to document the hundreds of kids that I teach every year (Mostly private requests and some group lessons from school programs). This way, I know exactly where I left off with last week's lesson and I don't have to waste time repeating that same drill or topic when they come back. Have your students keep a diary too! As a clinical professor at Ohio State University School of Medicine and Cleveland State University Graduate School, I have experienced that the students who don't take notes forget 65 percent of the previous lecture. Can you imagine the difficulties that I would have remembering the specifics on clients that return for lessons year after year? My pea brain would be in deep trouble as I forgot the specifics I previously taught. To ensure I don't leave anything to chance, I jot everything down in my portfolio and my pocket book.

Do not neglect the parent. Communicate with them as if they are taking the lesson; they will determine if Johnny will return a visit with you. Always remember, one of your main objectives in a lesson is to make connections with both the parent and the child.

Photo 4: A coach is assisting a mom buff her child's skis to help establish bonding.

Giving ample rewards. Besides verbal praises and high-five hand gestures and fist bumps, try giving stickers. The kids love stickers to put on their helmets and skis. You can find them in quantity at the dollar stores, or they be bought inexpensively online. Stickers can help to motivate your students, and those guests will seek you out for more stickers for their expanding collection. They are also visual merit badges that they have earned from being excellent on the slopes. Stickers can also build their self-esteem and confidence because you acknowledge their fine accomplishments. Child psychologists will say that all kids seek adult approval for their accomplishments.

Provide the child with homework, such as making pizza and French fries, by placing their bare feet on paper plates on a carpeted floor or with a little talcum powder underneath the plate on a hardwood, marble, or ceramic tile floor, and having them turning their toes inward and outward. Another fun drill to do is walking up the stairs with the toes pointed outward; this exercise helps with rotating the legs. They can also pretend that they are a stork and try to balance on each foot with the other foot raised. Have the parent actually time the child and see how long the child can accomplish the task. Many times, the parent will find that the coordination and strength of the leg is superior on one leg compared to the other. Ask them, "Communicate the results to me on your next lesson". This will help wet their appetite for the 'next lesson'.

Figure 5. A drawing of a skier in a wedge (Pizza) and another skier is in a parallel (French fries) platform. Note that the BOS for the wedge and parallel platform is hip width, which is the ideal distance between the boots for optimum balance.[46]

For those students who are returning the following year, I suggest the parent to build a low beam, like in gymnastics. Use a 4" x 4" inch x 8' timber, and use a 2" x 2" inch x 4' lumber attached to both ends of the beam for stability. During the summer, they can have the child walk up and down the low beam for balancing. Another excellent tool to recommend for enhancing balancing skills is the balancing board. This tool is especially useful for ages eight years old and older.

Photo 5. Gymnast on balance beam practicing fore/aft, lateral and vertical balance[46].

Expect the unexpected; kids do the darndest things. They think differently from adults, and some have cognitive, emotional, and physical challenges and insights that may surprise you. Do you know what to expect from a performance standpoint and some of the challenges that confront each age group? For more detail see chapters 2, 3, and 8. To be successful with your lessons, one of your highest priorities is bonding with children and developing trust. To help you to remember to always Konnect with children, try the following, EMPATHY:[39]

E = eye contact

M = muscles of facial expression

P = posture

A = affect

T = tone of voice

H = hearing the whole person

Y = your response

A supportive learning environment starts with doing and saying things that affect trust and integrity through honesty. In addition, develop a close rapport with your kids. Make every effort to be caring, kind, loving, polite, and fun filled.

Be attentive to the tone of voice. Psychologists have noted that kids are attracted to certain of types of tones. While genetics dictate how your voice sounds, train yourself to use a more soothing and warm tone, and alert yourself to never scream or use loud tones; this is especially true with children who have certain disorders.

Your posture reflects your attitude and confidence. Stand tall and erect when walking on the snow, and kneel to make eye contact when talking to the kids. Sprinkle some humor so that you don't appear stiff or stuffy.

Hear the whole person out. Kids want to be counted as important individual. Don't ignore what they have to say; many times, you can pick up cues that the reason they are not listening to you or learning what you are teaching them is something simple like a hearing problems About 15 percent of children have some type of hearing difficulty. Some helmet styles can also restrict sound. Solutions include speaking louder, speaking more slowly and clearly; checking if they have hearing aids and they are working properly; facing the child directly so that they can read your lips, not communicating in a noisy environment, and checking if their helmet design compromises their ability to hear at normal voice levels. Your responses should always be supportive. Accept their handicaps and find a solution to make it better. Empower the child to deal with the various issues by encouraging them with positive gestures when they respond positively to your instructions. Children need reinforcement. Do things repeatedly.

I would like to share a story close to my heart about developing bonding and trust. At the beginning of the ski season, I had a referral lesson from another parent. The student was a tiny five-year-old girl named Clementine. She was just adorable and was cuter than a bug's ear. She had big hazel eyes and a smile that could light up the world! During my introduction, her mom said that Clementine was afraid of speeds and heights. I explained where the parents could meet us after the lesson and where they could watch our lesson unfold. Clementine and I hopped around in the snow and played Green light/Red light and Simon Says.

I told her, "Her foot was the paintbrush, and she could paint a C and a J in the snow with her right foot, and then with the left foot." She then learned to make a pizza with the skis off, and then with the skis on. It was time to take Anna to a three-foot runoff.

This tiny munchkin was petrified to move. I immediately knew that I had to earn her *trust* through *bonding*. I said to Clementine, "I'm going to protect you as if you were my very own child, at *all* times." I proceeded to attach the ski harness onto her waist. She went down the runoff very slowly as I regulated her speed with the harness. We continued this task for the rest of the half-hour. We worked on the gliding wedge, focusing on the athletic stand. I fine-tuned the gliding wedge by making micro adjustments, (i.e., Making certain that her center of mass (COM) was directly over her base of support (BOS), the arches of the feet. In other words, always getting her re-centered on her skis for better balance. During that period, I began to understand her CAP profile: on a scale of 1 to 10 (*10* being the best), she had a cognitive development of 12, an affective development of 10, and a Physical development of 9.5. She was an attentive and exceptional listener and executed her drills with ease. I also asked her, "if she would like Coco the Monkey (Twelve long with extra-long arms with Velcro pads on the monkey's forearms to wrap around her neck) to ride on her back as we skied.

She said, "Yes, yes!"

I took Coco out of my backpack, which is filled with stuffed animals, puppets, magic tricks, tools, and she was so excited! The purpose of using monkey was to have her bend from the hips about thirty degrees to get her back slanted slightly into the athletic stand. Also, I taught her, "Knees ahead of the toes. Nose ahead of the toes." I told her, "If you stand upright, Coco will slide down her back, but if you tilt your back a little forward by having your head and nose forward, Coco will be able to hang on." I told her that is how you need to be - in an athletic stand at all times when skiing.[7]

With the skis off, we worked on putting pressure on the inside edge of the boot and flattening the other boot while in a small wedge stance. We also worked on pointing the toes in the direction of the turns (Called rotary control[29]). We did the same drills with the skis on. By the end of the fifty-five-minute lesson, she was able to link the C-turns. Each step of the way, we did high-fives. I gave her verbal praises, and lots of fist bumps. I told her if she came back for another lesson, we would try a five-foot, a ten-foot, a twenty-foot runoff, but she would not go on the chairlift just yet - until *she* told me we could.

I said, "Clementine, you are the *boss*. I will do what you want."

During the second half of the hour, we went higher and higher on the slope. At the end of the hour, she was making linked wedge turns! I asked Clementine, "What do you think about skiing?"

She said, "I had so much fun. I want to bring my best friend with me."

Her prized reward was selecting a sticker (Butterflies) for her helmet! I gave her homework on balance by having her pretend that she was a flamingo that lifted one leg while balancing on the other for five minutes daily. Her parents were tickled pink and I was booked with her every week for the rest of the season.

On subsequent lessons, we focused on four things (1) the Skills Concept Model (See page 51), (2) the Five Fundamentals of Skiing Model (See page 61), (3) being balanced through the four phases of the turns, (See page 57) and skiing safely (See figure 11-13,16, and chapter 4). By her fifth lesson, Clementine had progressed to being able to follow me down all the advanced slopes (Black diamond) slopes, making beautiful, controlled parallel C-turns. Both of her parents were thrilled with her outcome, and I was invited to Clementine's sixth birthday party at their home with her friends that summer. That's the power of bonding and trust!

Photo 6. Young girl expressing happiness and showing one thumb's up because she followed her coach down an advanced (Black diamond) slope making controlled, parallel C-turns, Successful coaching result in exponential results and rewards like creating a huge smile on this girl's face.

There are key qualities that are common denominators in all outstanding teachers and coaches:

A. Qualities of great coaching:

- Know the ABCs of *bonding.*
- The ability to create *trust.*
- The ability to *impartially* evaluate a student with nonjudgmental feedback.
- Know how to motivate a child.
- Create a positive learning environment.
- Be always thoughtful, considerate, gentle, caring and kind.
- Always develop memorable and fun learning activities
- Provide accurate and meaningful comments.
- Provide a closure that answers the questions "What did you do?" "How did you do it?" "Why did you do it?" and "Where did you do it?"
- Be creative and imaginative for fun games, and use ski tools to enhance their learning experience. Try learning to be a magician[26,38] or a ventriloquist[44] to generate a lot of excitement and fun.

18

- Know how to create unique and creative lessons specific to each child and not cookie-cutter lessons that are used with every child, year after year. Read up on horse-riding Training[35, 45, 51] and introduce it into your lesson plans for horse lovers (More can be read in chapter 1).
- For new-hire and returning coaches, do a lot of shadowing and take educational clinics from an educational staff member.
- Know how to assess and provide lessons specific to the student's cognitive, affective, and physical developmental states. Don't neglect the nerve development with each group because they regulate how the muscles work. And affects coordination
- Determine the type of learners they are.
- Recognize the child's limitations, whatever they are.
- Teach the various ways of speed control (See discussions in chapter 4 and figs. 11-13, 16, 17. Knowing how to assess if they learned the consequences of being out of speed control (Fears and physical, mental, and emotional injuries); teach how to correct for runaway speed (See chapter 4, under "Bag of Tricks").
- Know how to involve the parents' in each stage of the learning process.
- Always ask your customers for honest feedback to continually improve one's skills.
- Review key points used in your lesson and encourage your student to write them down in a notebook or diary when the child goes home.
- Always follow the motto "always be prepared for the unexpected."
- Parents relish photographs of their precious child. If you want to step-it-up a notch, invest in a sports cam and take videos of the kid's performance and share it with his\her parents.

B. Assessing the Child:

- Know the limitations of their ski equipment.
- Ensure they have a helmet and goggles and they are properly fit.
- Ensure they are dressed appropriately for the weather conditions.
- Ensure the skis and poles are the correct length for their skill level.
- Ensure the right boot and left boot is on the left foot. Are the boots the correct size and fit, snug, and buckled appropriately?

- Accurately assess the child\s cognitive, affective, and physical developmental stages when establishing realistic goals during lesson-plan creation. [5,16]
- Know what you can expect, performance wise, for the different age groups (See chapter 8).
- Know the challenges (Problems) you can encounter with each group (See chapters 2 and 3). There is a correlation between the amount of lesson structure need by the child and the amount expected by the parent by each age group (See figure 8) and the amount of fun required. For example, for younger children, parents need to understand that the young child does better with less structure and information and more fun activities. On the other end of the spectrum, the parents of older children need to understand that the child does better with more structure and information and needs to adjust the amount and quality of fun to a level that maintains their interest in the lesson. This relationship between amount of structure and information and the amount of fun needed by the child and parent is discussed in greater detail in chapter 3 under The Five Fundamentals of the Skiing Model.[46]

Here is an example of structured problem-solving:

1. Defining the Challenge:
   - What is the current situation?
   - Why is this a challenge?
   - What would it look like if the challenge was solved; and how would you know?
   - What are the obstacles to solving the challenge?

2. Solving the Challenge:
   - What can you try first to solve the challenge?
   - Let's try it.
   - Did that solve the challenge? If not, what did you learn from the failure?
   - Do you have a stepping stone or alternative way to address the challenge?

3. Other considerations:
   - Is your lesson plan focused on the right amount of structured, technical information and the right amount of fun and games?

- Is your goal an idealistic goal[5, 46] or a realistic goal that meets both the parent and child's needs? See chapter 8 for more discussion on realistic goals for each age group and the challenges you can expect.
- Has your teaching exceeded Customer Satisfaction?[27]
- Each student brings a unique blend of characteristics to your lesson. These characteristics are based on many factors and make up the student's profile.[33, 46]
- How does the child process the information (Cognitive) and what prompts the student to learn?
- How does the child's emotional (Affective) development relate to their motivation? Also, the child's beliefs, attitudes, and values also help determine the emotional development.
- What is the child's state of physical development?
- What is the child's dominant learning style? Is the child a watcher, doer, thinker, or feeler?
- What are some of the challenges that you may encounter for each age group? See chapters 2 and 3 for more details.
- What are the child's goals for accomplishment?
- Determine how much structure and how much fun you should have with that particular child and parent (See figure 13).

By evaluating the student's ability to learn, we are in a better position to develop a meaningful learning experience and teach the whole child. Be mindful that your lesson plan should be student centered.

When planning your lesson plan, consider the PSIA CAP Model (See figure 3).[2-5. 13, 33, 46 47] The PSIA CAP Model can be very helpful when creating your lesson plan. Pay attention to the early phase of your meeting with your student. Try to analyze the student's profile to better understand a child's expectation and what they'll be able to accomplish on the hill. Also, this provides a foundation for better lesson planning. This important topic is covered extensively covered in chapters 2 and 8.

Student's Profile[33, 46]

Cognitive. Cognitive growth involves an individual's ability to process information obtained through experiences. It is their point of view, based on their observation. How you communicate with the kids depends on their cognitive development:

- How they process the information in their brain
- How they express themselves
- How they reason

Affective. Affective growth involve kids' humor, self-identity, self-esteem, play, moral values. Do not underestimate the importance of assessing the child's developmental stage to create a successful lesson plan.

Physical. Physical growth involves how kids move; muscle and skeletal development (Motor control, balance, coordination, center of mass, large and small muscle movements and coordination, being tall or small, skinny or overweight; three-years-old or thirteen-years-old can be deceiving when it comes to physical maturation and coordination).

As a coach, you need to figure out your student's cognitive development. For example, communication with kids is a real art. Does a three-year-old student know what you mean by a left turn or a right turn? Never assume that they do; many don't. The tiny tots (Below age five) seem to know colors much better. So, why not place a red sticker on their right-hand glove and a green sticker on their left-hand glove? Now, you can instruct them to make a green turn or a red turn. Avoid placing stickers on the toes of their boots because kids tend to look down at the stickers. I cannot stress enough that as a kid's coach, you must be creative and imaginative. Keep it simple, keep it short, and keep the instruction clear and understandable by checking how they perceived your instructions. Also, by making it *fun*. "Be Brief, be Brilliant, be gone!"

Everyone needs to be motivated. How do you motivate a child to do something that they are not in the mood to do, fear of doing, or are disinterested in doing? Your enthusiasm for the sport, your passion for coaching, and your commitment to exceeding customer satisfaction will go a long way.

To succeed you need to be creative and have an insightful imagination. Remember, as a snow sport instructor, you're in the *entertainment* business. You are there to create *fun* and *excitement*! It begins with your mental attitude, which can then motivate your behavior.

For example, during my hour-and-a half drive to the ski resorts from my home, I remind myself, "It's show time!" This allows me to mentally prepare myself who I'll be that day. Am I to be a clown? A magician? A ventriloquist with one of my dozens of puppets? What color and style hair wig should I wear? If you are gifted with a beautiful voice, serenade your students while riding up on the chairlift. If you have any musical talents, jam with them by playing the harmonica or kazoo. We all spent a lot of time creating those a- ha moments over the years perfecting these different activities. Use those priceless creative resources of yours to add to your bag of tricks to help formulate these memorable moments for our students.

To illustrate how powerful this can be, I will tell you a story about a three-year-old girl, Abigayle, who came for her first ski lesson. She and her dad were at the ski school desk to book a lesson with me. I realized that she was stuttering whenever she tried to talk. I realized I needed to calm her anxiety about skiing to try and reduce the stuttering during her ski lesson. While on both my knees, I told Abigayle, "I have magical powers to keep her safe and to have tons and tons of fun on the snow." I showed her my powers by demonstrating two different magical tricks. Two red-colored balls, one in each of my hand, disappeared in front of her very eyes, only to find them in her ski-jacket; The second magic trick was a disappearing blue ball in a black bag that vanished when I said, "Abracadabra, disappear!" She examined the bag thoroughly, and to her amazement the blue ball was nowhere to be found. She was in awe. She took my hand and walked out to the snow while I carried her skis. We hopped on one leg on flat land, pretending we had a sprained ankle from her bicycle accident the previous week. The purpose was for weight transfer to one leg to practice balancing on one leg. Then after a one-minute drill, we switched to the other leg. I quickly noticed that Abigayle was more coordinated and stronger on her left leg as compared to the right leg. I asked her, "Are you right-handed or left-handed?" What do you think? Then we started with a static drill by making smiley faces in the snow with her right boot and then with her left boot, to familiarize her with edging control.[46] I demonstrated the perfect pizza (Being hip width) and then, French fries. We went to a five-foot runoff and glided down in a wedge. During this time, I was able to asses her CAP development; 0 to 10 (*10* being the best). Her cognitive development was a 10, her effective development was an 8, and her physical development was a 7 or 8. Toward the end of the one-hour lesson, we moved higher on the hill, six-foot, seven-foot, and ten-foot runoffs - all the while assessing her movement skills and how they affected the skis. Whenever I saw a technical error, I informed Abigayle how we could do it better without being negative. I sprinkled a little humor periodically by making lots of kid's jokes to get her to relax and have fun during the lesson. She did gliding-wedge runs with slightly larger pizza (Wedge changeups) at the bottom to get her to a stop. I get a little concerned with this method of stopping because too big of a wedge will cause their COM to be behind the BOS, which results in being out of balance,[29] thus causing imbalance. I prefer J-turns for the purpose of going down the hill and making a J-turn to go up-hill to come to a stop. Abigayle couldn't do it, so we stuck to what she could do with a larger wedge on a less steep hill with a longer run. This technique later proved to be useful for emergency stops.

She completed her lesson by being able to make slight directional turns in control. She was tickled pink, and we went into the ski lodge and commented to her dad what, where, how and why we did those drills. I asked Abigayle what she thought of her first ski lesson. She said, "I loved it. It was better than riding my bicycle!"

I gave the smiling Abigayle homework on rotary control[46] by doing pizza and French fries on paper plate under each foot on the carpet to maximize the ease of turning of the plates. She received candy kisses for her excellent performance (With the approval of her dad).

I did the second magic trick, the disappearing nickel in the box, and found the lost nickel in her ski jacket pocket. I was booked every weekend with Abigayle for the rest of the season. Guess what? Her parents noticed that Abigayle was not stuttering!

Photo 7. A three-year-old girl showing excitement and joy after completing her first ski-lesson. This positive of overwhelming happiness is the result of good coaching.

The ability to motivate children effectively depends on their affective development

- How they relate to their peers
- How they relate to adults
- How they think about themselves
- Their personality and emotional makeup
- Their social skills

A child's self-identity is shaped, in large part, by social interactions with others, and their development of moral values is closely related to the development of self-identity. Play is what children do best! Play is fun, but it also is a critical part of their learning process. Through play, children learn how to adapt to their surroundings, how to socialize with others and how to compete.

The steps to analyzing the child's affective development is not easy. You need to look for clues based on their outward behavior and by asking questions to assess their inner feelings. For example, you can ask,

- Do you have sisters or brothers?
- How old are they?
- Who's your best friend?

- What do you both like to do for fun?
- Do you have any pets?
- What's your favorite TV show?

You can begin to see the level of their social skills, their ability to communicate, their ability to express their emotions, and their fears and concerns about the snow sport.

How the children learn the appropriate skiing movements depends primarily on their physical and cognitive developments. An awareness of children's physical development will help explain why and how children move the way that they move. Your goal is to develop effective, efficient movements in our students as they learn and develop. Effective movement patterns are often quite different for children than for adults. Children develop from top to the bottom and from the core outward. They tend to use the larger muscles rather than their smaller muscles, which are less refined in their movements. The brain is their control center, which fires the signals to the muscles but at a slower rate than an adult. It is especially important that we exercise patience and repetition when coaching these movements to children.

Consider how the child's body is proportioned, which will affect their balance point on the skis.

- What is the developmental state of the child's neuro-muscular development?
- How much muscle strength does the child have?
- How much spatial awareness do they possess?
- Does the child have the ability to use different parts of the body separately? Can they maneuver the right half of the body separately from the left half? This coordination skill is difficult with the tiny tots.
- What kind and how much coordination and timing of movements does the child possess?

You may also wish to consider the following PSIA CAP developmental stages:

- Children are able to use large muscle groups but may not be able to skillfully use small muscle groups yet. Gross motor skills and movements develop first (It may be easier to run and gallop than to use a pencil).

- One sided movement is easier than cross-lateral movements (It is harder to swing the right arm and left leg at the same time as compared to moving one arm forward and the other arm in the opposite direction).
- A child's head is usually larger in proportion to his body compared to an adult. This makes the child's center of mass (COM) slightly higher in his body and may account for the differences in his skiing stance. The child may hunch over to lower the COM and use the upper body as a lever arm to assist in rotating the feet and skis.

Don't be surprised if a five-year old girl has, in general, more advanced physical development than a seven-year-old boy. Kids develop at different rates and at different times during their developmental stages of growth. A lot of this physical development can be enhanced by genetic factors, environmental factors, and educational factors. It has been my experience that when I receive a kid who is a gymnast, the child tends to have better balance, coordination of moving body parts, and muscular strength than someone who is not athletically inclined. The CAP Model is discussed in greater detail in chapters 6, 8 and 9.

Finally, a sought-after instructor tends to follow a business model[27] (My modified version [See figure 6] of Deer Valley Ski Resort's business model). They have a unified approach to pleasing all customers.

BUSINESS MODEL

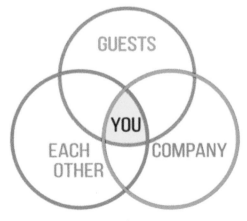

Figure 6. Modified business model[27] with overlapping of the 3 circles

It became apparent to me while teaching at Deer Valley Ski Resort, in Utah, one of the many reasons they could tout their outstanding ski instructor staff: their commitment to a business model. You need to define who your customer is: the GM of the resort, the supervisor, the owners of the ski resort, the many chefs, the bus boys, the chair-lift operators, the custodial staff, your fellow instructors, your students, their parents? Believe it or not, they are *all* your customers! So, take care of each other, the company, and guests; they are all critical to your profession. Treat everyone with full respect, courtesy, dignity. In turn, you will have a more cohesive unit, all working together with a common goal - to exceed Customer Satisfaction.[27]

While I was working at the prestigious Cleveland Clinic Foundation in Ohio, the CEO stated that as competitive as the work environment was (e.g., Medical staff were provided only a one-year contract, which needed to be renewed each year), we all needed to work as a *unit*. As we have all learned with the recent COVID-19 pandemic, we are all in this together. So, working together and helping your fellow colleagues to become the best that they can be, is one of your responsibilities.

Share your daily lessons with your colleagues - the good, the bad, and the ugly. Not every lesson is a smashing success. Ask colleagues what they could have done with the unsuccessful lessons to make them great. Here are some challenging problems that I have encountered during my career as an instructor:

Challenge: A six-year-old boy did not stay focused on the lesson; his mind kept wandering off and he kept talking about many other things that were not related to the task at hand.

Solution: Kindly asked his parent whether or not I needed to know anything special about Johnny. They reported he had a mild case of ADHD. That being said, I kept the tasks short, simple, and fun. I kept him actively moving, talking less, and skiing more. I allowed him to take the lead to do a movement and praised him for the excellent job. We played a lot of games, such as Simon says, cops and robbers, and red Light-green light.

I surmised the student did not connect with the other coach, which made the child disinterested in what the coach had to say.

Challenge: Lack of discipline in the group lesson. Everyone wanted to do their own thing; too much group talking.

Solution: You need to take command. Children need to have structure. They need to have boundaries. But, don't be a drill sargent; instead, be a sea captain that guides his crew to find hidden treasures. Sometimes, a time-out is necessary to correct a discipline problems. Sometimes, it is because the Hierarchy of Needs are not being met (e.g., Hungry, thirsty, needs to go to the bathroom, sleepy). Sometimes, it is due to ADD, ADHD, or autism, or even types 1 and 2 diabetic conditions, which include with hypoglycemia (Low blood sugar). Many of these clinical conditions can lead to cognitive impairments and stress disorders. Collecting information from the parents is important when trying to figure out disarray on the slope. Having full class participation and having all of them give their input on how they feel the lesson went can help. Having fun things that they want can always help. Sometimes you simply need a time-out session!

Challenge: Losing your child or returning him/her late from your lesson.

Solution: Try to avoid these situations. Do not hesitate to apologize. Some of the larger ski resorts have GPS for each of their kids (Group lessons) and can track them (i.e., Going through paths with different outlets when going through the forest or trees). If you do not have any such tracking gadgets, be explicit where to meet when the child gets lost. In addition, depending on the policies of your ski resort, you might want to immediately call the front desk or their parents.

Problem: The three- or six- year-old child is constantly crying.

Solution: Are the hierarchy of needs being met?[13, 16, 31, 50] Did you ask the child what is bothering them or why is there so much sadness or unhappiness? Is the child's lesson scheduled during their normal nap time? Have you tried other methods, such as scrapping the lesson and just doing snow angels or building a snowman, or having a snowball fight (Being careful not to hurt the child's face, eyes, head; safer yet, why not just let the child pelt you with snowballs?). I always carry small bottles of bubble-blowing materials. We blow bubbles outside on the snow until the cows come home; this trick always works. Your job is to be creative and motivate the child to like and want to ski (See figure 4).

Let me tell you a story that didn't start out so well. This story is about Memory, a three-year-old girl, who came for her first ski lesson. She and her dad were at the ski school front desk to book a lesson with me. I realized she was afraid and did not want to go on to the snow. There also appeared to be separation anxiety involved because she had her arms wrapped tightly around her dad's leg. She squeezed his leg tighter when he urged her to go out and have fun. Soon she had tears. I told Memory, "I was Pineapple Herb, and that I have magical powers to always keep her safe at all times," and I promised her she would have tons of fun on the snow." I did three different magical tricks (Changing the color of a handkerchief in front of her very own eyes, a disappearing nickel in a tiny box that was later found in her ski jacket (I let her keep the nickel), and a disappearing pea under one of the three walnuts that was never found). She was awe-struck! To my surprise, she took my hand and we walked out to the snow without a whimper.

I also asked her, "Would like Freddie the Frog to ride on her back as we ski?"

She said, "Yes!"

Boy, was she excited! The purpose of using Freddie the Frog was to entertain her on the snow and, more importantly, to have her bend from the hips to achieve a slight angle (e.g.,About 30 degrees) on her back to help achieve an athletic stance for better balance on the moving skis.[7] I told her, "If you stand upright, Freddie will slide down her back; but if you tilt her back forward a little, Freddie will be able to hang on for the ride."

I explained to the dad where we would meet after the lesson and where he could watch our lesson unfolded. We were hopping in the snow like crazy jack rabbits. We then lifted one foot up while balancing on the other foot, pretending we were Flamingos. Next, we went sliding down the hill slowly (With a ski harness attached to her waist) with her feet making a pizza of various sizes.

I told Memory, "I'm tired of Pizza, let's make French Fries and go down the little hill." At the end, I asked Memory, "What did you think about your first ski lesson?"

She said, "It was a lot of fun. It was better than riding my bike!"

We walked in hand in hand into the lodge, where I had my 12 pages of stickers and told Memory to choose one for her excellent skiing on the hill. I told Memory, "I am so proud of your accomplishments." I *always* reward children with stickers for their efforts and successes. She picked a unicorn horse sticker and placed it on the front of her helmet. I was booked with Memory for the rest of the season.

The point of this story is that an instructor must be creative, be able to analyze and reduce or alleviate children's anxieties, and provide fun games that will promote the proper body movements to get those skis to turn in control. *Fun* is the name of the game; having the kids do fun games without them knowing that they are learning skiing movements with their bodies to get the skis to respond appropriately, is the mission of every good coach. Every coach should follow the *unwritten code,* ensuring every child has a happy smile at the end of a fun-filled lesson."

Photo 8: Be prepared to expect the unexpected; always be prepared to address the issues and challenges and bring on happy faces. Not every day is a walk in the park; this three-year-old girl, an excellent skier, is having a bad hair day with her new instructor.

Challenge: A reckless kid who just wants to bomb the hill at high speeds without turning.

Solution: Ask yourself, "Is the high speed due to not being able to turn properly under control?" In that case, it is the instructor's fault. Re-evaluate how you taught that lesson; modify your approach, and check if they understand the consequences (More on that scenario in chapter 4). Or is it that they want the thrill of speed? Stress the importance of speed control and continue to work on turning completely.

Challenge: A teenager is reluctant to do a demonstration of a movement in front of the class.

Solution: This age group is more socially oriented. They do not want to be singled out for fear that their self-image and self-esteem will negatively influenced by their peers. Instead, you might want to pair them up with their best friend and let one of them volunteer to demonstrate the movement and the other try to execute the movement. Listen to what they are saying and observe how they are doing the maneuvers. Then reverse the role (i.e., The one who did the demo, now becomes the executor). For this type of scenario to work, your demonstration must be perfect and your verbal presentation must be precise and clear. You can also select a student that did the demonstration "perfectly". A picture is worth a thousand words and is priceless. Tell the student how outstanding that movement was and it was textbook illustration on how to do it. Tell the student to please show the class how it should be done. Always, always, always give positive encouragement, reinforcement, accolades to help build their self-esteem and confidence. Every one of us seeks approval and praises from others, especially children. As they always say, "Sugar always works much better than vinegar."

In the pursuit of spreading this handbook of knowledge, tips, experiences, and passion to our follow snow sport instructors, I would like to share my version of collaborating with others to facilitate a better working environment. This is my concoction of a business model: The HOPE philosophy:

Helping

Other

People

Everyday

This will help enable all of our coaches to be on the same page to help deliver services that meet the customer needs, and better yet, exceed customer satisfaction!

At the end of each chapter, I will provide golden nuggets (*Treasure of gold*a) to stimulate your thought process to help create a successful lesson that exceeds customer satisfaction.

 Knowing how to Konnect with kids is paramount to successful outcomes when teaching children of all ages. Master the techniques of bonding and developing trust with the parent and child.

---

a Used with permission from Microsoft

CHAPTER 2

Developing a Strong Foundation—Assessing a Student's Profile

Before you can even develop your lesson plan for the day, you first need to accurately assess the student's profile[33, 46] (More is discussed in chapter 3). What are the child's needs and goals? What stage of cognitive, affective, and physical (PSIA CAP) development (See figure 3) is the child at currently? What motivates them? What type of learner are they? More of the CAP model is elaborated in chapters 8 and 9.

The CAP Model[2 -5, 13, 14, 33, 46, 47]

Cognitive: How kids think, process the information, follow instructions.

Affective: How kids feel (Humor, self-identity, play, ability to follow rules, moral values, competitive in nature, emotional development).

Physical: How kids move; nerve, muscle, and skeletal muscle development (Motor control, balance, coordination, center of mass, large and small muscle movements and coordination).

Each age group has different rates of PSIA CAP development, and assessing the profile of a child can be daunting. Your time with your student is limited during the introduction phase, and the information gathered from the parent might be inflated when it comes to the actual skills the child has on the snow. To accurately determine the profile of your student requires lots of astute observations, ask lots of questions of the parent and the child and making your own judgements when you finally get on the snow.

Learning Styles[16, 33, 46]

People learn with different learning styles.[16,33, 46] According to psychologists, there are Five Elements of Learning: physiological, environmental, sociological, physiological, and emotional. There are many learning styles (Verbal, visual, musical/auditory, physical/kinesthetic, combination, solitary, social, logical/mathematical). However, these can be simplified and boiled down to the VAK Model[46] (See figure 7). It should be emphasized that the different styles of learning may not translate to learning the material; it simply means, according to many published reports, students prefer to receive information for processing in a specific way (e.g., Visually, or hearing the message, or feeling how to do a task). The primary and secondary learning styles will vary depending on the activity involved. The bottom line is, don't get too hung up on just learning styles because people learn by various methods depending on the circumstances. It is much better to think of a student having a toolbox that contains ways to think, memorize, and employ a task. However, there are many learning specialists that recommend you hold on to a framework of the different learning styles so you can provide a rich, varied presentation when you present a new movement, activity, or skill.

Understand the VAK Model[46] (See figure 7) when crafting your lesson plans: the three pathways by which a signal gets to the brain.

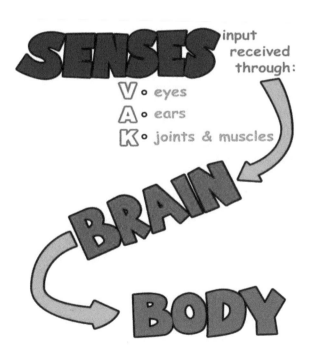

Figure 7 VAK model: a learning style[46]

V = *Visual.* These individuals learn best when charts, graphics, images, drawings, and pictures/photographs are used instead of words. They store information in the brain as a picture and need to watch and mimic movements. They look for good demonstrations so they can mimic the body movements.

A = *Auditory.* These individuals like spoken words, preferring lectures and discussions over pictures. They store information as a running commentary and need to know the how and why. These kids tend to like to listen to music, sing, and listen to the radio.

K = *Kinesthetic.* These individuals like tactile processes; they prefer to create concrete personal experiences and like to process the information by recreating and practicing. They learn best by doing activities to experience how it feels. Ask your students, "What did you feel when doing that movement?"

With this type of learners, the results are:

- I hear, but I forget...
- I see, and I remember...
- I do, and I understand...

Another approach to categorizing learning styles is to follow the Kolb Learning Model.[28] The sequence of learning lends to the actual blending of the sequence if you placed them in a round circle (See figure 8):

Feeler. These types of students need to feel the movement and activity they are doing. So, as a coach, you need to help them what, where, how to feel the movements. Remember, kinesthetic implies feeling outside the body, while proprioceptive means feeling within the body. This is the same with the kinesthetic discussion above.

Watcher. These types of students are visual learners and want to see how you do it (Accurate and precise demonstrations are mandatory). These visual learners target attention to specific areas (What body parts move, how the skis respond to the movements) and prefer views from different angles. Drawing in the snow, using your hands, or using metaphors will often provide the necessary picture they need for their brain to process. The same applies on what we discussed above under Visual in the VAK model.

Thinker. These types of students ask many how and why questions and learn best by using cognitive abilities. They want details, so you should provide a rational as to why, how, when, and where? They prefer a direct dialogue with them to do a verbal and/or visual exchange. Depending on their age, they can deal with abstract concepts. While keeping the instructions simple, do ask your students, "Why are we doing that drill ?" or if I do this body movement incorrectly, what are the effects on the skis?"

Doer. These types of student want the big picture and need to know what is necessary; they will attempt to do self-discovery on how to do it, with proper guidance from you. They will do a lot of experimentation and discover by trial and error for the desired outcome. These kids usually want to be first to go.

It should be stated that intrinsic feedback should be a supplement to learning styles. Intrinsic feedback is the student's inner voice. In addition to giving extrinsic feedback, instructors need to ask students to share what they think and feel about what they are doing. For example, the student did a task and the coach said, "Good job", or "That was awesome." However, the child's inner voice is saying, "I don't understand what I just did. It doesn't feel awesome." Intrinsic feedback is especially important to Feelers and tor affective development of children as this becomes a reference point. In addition to giving feedback, instructors should ask the students, how they felt it went.

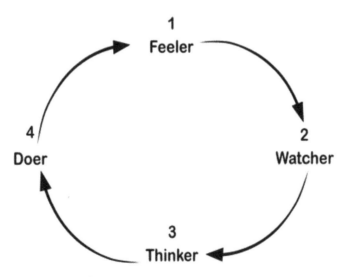

Figure 8. Kolb Learning Model: a sequence of learning[28]

The Four Principles of Learning[16, 33, 46]

When organizing your presentations, keep in mind the four principles of learning: *structure, effort, active learning,* and *relevance.*

Structure: Organize and clarify the information. Pay attention to how the information is organized to understand the big picture and grasp the main ideas. Don't be bogged down with superfluous details. Keep it simple. Ask yourself, "What is the main idea being communicated? Why are we here?"

Effort: Engage with the material. Test your comprehension by writing down what you want them to learn in your own words without looking at the source material. Strengthen neural connections by using spaced repetitions. Keep similar ideas in your working memory longer to make them stick. Know your material thoroughly and know how to adapt to various situations.

Active Learning: Use what you learned. Make abstract concepts more concrete by applying them to your daily coaching, and make them a part of your life.

Relevance: Have a good reason for learning. Consume information that is relevant to your life and to your skiing. Focus on information and techniques of movements that are current and can be used now, effectively and efficiently. The trick is knowing how to present the information in a way that the kids can comprehend and execute.

Instructor's Profile[16, 33, 46]

In addition to assessing the student's profile, you should also assess the instructor's profile. How much knowledge and experience do you have coaching kids? How motivated are you to teach the young children? How passionate are you in creating outstanding lessons and ones that are above and beyond their expectations? View the student's profile and instructor's profile as a continuous ongoing partnership. See chapter 3 for more discussion on the instructor's profile.

Your accountability is very important during your development as a professional. Your knowledge and skills should be challenged periodically; your ability to teach at different levels and ages and on different terrains should be reviewed (e.g., Some of the larger ski resorts have coaches wear GPS to monitor if they are on the green, blue, or black terrain for the beginner, intermediate, or advance zone. Some resorts have the luxury of having PSIA examiners and trainers (Out of uniform) skiing all over the mountain resort, observing coaches' teaching skills and how they interact with their students. Part of being accountable is also being at work on time. Nothing is more frustrating to the snow sport's front desk than an instructor failing to be present for an assignment or refusing to accept a kid that wants to learn a special skill, like being in the terrain park. There are many ways of checking for accountability; and more monitoring is necessary to check your dependability for your job. What can you do? You can check if you have done your homework to excel in this profession. When was the last time that you got feedback from your customer? Your students depend on you for accurate feedback to make improvements in their skiing. You, too, need feedback to improve your skills: the good, the bad, and the ugly comments. Make it a practice to ask for feedback from your students (And parents). At the closure of every lesson, I always ask my students, "What did you like about today's lesson? What games and activities did you like and why? What didn't you like and why? Did you have fun? What was the best part of today's event? Would you come back again for another lesson with me?"

Another thought that you should consider: are *you* a great coach, and how do you know that you are at the top of your game? In my opinion, there are eight ways to tell and you can candidly ask yourself the question:

When you're on top of your game:

- Were your skiing goals realistic[16] and not idealistic[16,] and could the student easily achieve them?
- Did you receive positive comments, even accolades from the parents or students?
- Did your clients come back for a private lesson?
- Did the parents or students broadcast your great teaching skills to their friends to help expand your client base?
- Did you receive any monetary tips for your excellent services?
- Did you see signs of excitement, such as big smiles, enthusiasm to go back out and practice what they learned, and jubilation on their faces after their lesson?

- Do you frequently get asked by your fellow ski instructors on how to teach a particular movement or what tools to use when coaching a particular age group how to turn or what kind of games would work best for balance on a steeper slope?
- Do your coaches ask you if they can shadow you when you teach a child in one of your many lessons?
- Have you received any accolades from the ski resort (e.g., Ski Instructor of the Year, MVP Coach, or Most Dedicated Teacher?
- Have you been invited to be a member of the Educational Staff, who help train the new hires and returning ski instructors.

Diversification is also important for a coach's growth in becoming an excellent instructor—the ability to teach different age groups (Three- to six- year-old, seven – to ten- year-old, and eight- to eighteen-year-old), different zones (Beginner, intermediate, advanced, expert), and different terrains (Moguls, green, blue, black). It is common to observe many instructors gravitating to only certain age groups or certain performance zones during their entire career. Your value increases as you diversify your skills and knowledge by getting certified in different disciplines (PSIA Level 1, 2, 3, Children's Specialist, Senior Specialist, Adaptive, Cross-country, telemarketing, Free style, Snow-boarding).

Hone or learn new language skills to connect with your students with different ethnicities. I know a little Spanish, Japanese, and Hawaiian languages, and I use every opportunity to communicate to Hispanic-speaking, Japanese-speaking and Hawaiian-speaking students. I can tell you that this diversity has helped me to connect with many students. As it has been said many times, "Get on the Bandwagon, and don't be left behind!"

Flexibility with your schedule is another hallmark of a good coach. Can you be available on nonscheduled days or nights to accommodate a special field trip of kids (Boy Scouts/girl Scouts, church groups, inner-city school kids who do not have the resources to go skiing, homeschoolers, or slightly disadvantaged children)? When the ski school is shorthanded, are you willing to change ski boots and equipment to snowboard boots and board to help fill the needed gap required for a waiting lesson? Many times, there are the necessary amount of ski instructors, but they cannot teach the different ages or the different performance zones. Are you able to assist in the rental department when needed? On several occasions, I have volunteered to be a scanner to allow people with season passes or daily tickets to access the slopes. I have even volunteered to be a lift operator when the resort was short of help. Be flexible and help out the front desk, which is trying its best to meet the customer's needs.

Flexibility also means when you have idle time, you might want to ask management if you can help out in other way, such as assisting with cleaning up the ski hut or sprinkling salt on slippery sidewalks. On your own you can clean up a food spill that just occurred on the outside tables because of the high winds, help someone who is having difficulty getting into their ski bindings, or get the necessary paperwork for registration for an equipment ski rental or forms for the different children's programs.

Other items that fall under flexibility include adjusting quickly to varying bad weather conditions, adjusting your lesson plans when the current one is not working, and changing your tactics when you are confronted with a child who is having a bad-hair day.

These extended efforts will help enhance the business model you need to support.

 Recognizing a student's profile and understanding their learning styles, along with knowing how to fulfill their needs and goals, will lead to more successful lessons. Developing a strong student-instructor-partnership is paramount.

CHAPTER 3

Developing a Strong Foundation—
Organizing the Lesson Plan

Children just want to have *FUN!*

Children want to be excited and stimulated by what they are doing, and of course, skiing on the snow can be just that. When you are introducing a new task or activity, if the information is not fun or meaningful, it may not stimulate the child, and their arousal level may drop into the boredom zone. Be creative and innovative, and do whatever you can to grab their interest and attention. More on the importance of coach creativity is discussed in chapter 1 on bonding and trust.

Photo 9. Ski instructor entertaining a three-year-old boy with a hand puppet for entertainment and to build bonding and trust.[16]

You can enhance the way you present this new information by stimulating the interest of the child to bring it back into optimal zone for learning. Remember, your lesson plan should always be student centered.

Better Learning Mechanics[46]

When developing your creative lesson plan, there are three things to keep in mind to achieve better learning mechanics and outcomes: *mechanics*, *techniques*, and *tactics*.

Mechanics (the "what"). This refers to what basic body movements are necessary to get essential actions of the skis to respond. This basic principle applies at all times, regardless of the terrain, snow conditions, pitch of the slope, speed of the descent, and age of the person.

Techniques (the "how"). This refers to the methods you teach to apply the mechanics of skiing to get the skis to move in the snow. Different techniques provide movement options for how skiers react or are affected by the actions of the skis on the snow.

Tactics (the "why"). This refers to the strategic choices you choose in your lessons to achieve your goal. Decisions are based on intent, knowledge, and level of performance of your student within the context of the skiing environment. Your kids may choose to adjust the turn shape, speed, line, timing, or technique to accommodate the many other factors, such as snow conditions, terrain, fear factor, steepness of the hill.

When teaching a new skill, always start on a lower terrain. It should be emphasized that the progression of information you provide should be clear, concise, and in the proper sequence for more effective and efficient learning. Your time is limited on the slope so, do not add "fillers" (Unnecessary information that do not pertain to the current topic) in your lessons. For example:

- Minimize the addition of tasks and drills that do not apply to the movements and skills that you are trying to cover. A couple of drills that apply and can be practiced multiple times by your students are better than many that may be meaningless to the goals at hand.

- Do not add materials that have no particular bearing on the mechanics and techniques you are teaching. I especially find inexperienced coaches that add extra drills because they don't have sure-fire activities that can get the job done efficiently and effectively.
- Finally, do not stand on the hill with endless explanations; many of the kids have already been in regular school classes all day and do not want any more lectures! In my opinion, if you know your materials thoroughly, you should be succinct enough to present a task in less than 30 seconds. As one 12-year-old student told me, "This sport is called skiing, dude, and not talking, so let's move and have fun!"

Our job as instructors/coaches require us to make hundreds of decisions as we guide children in the learning process. We need to organize and present our materials in a fashion to obtain the most out of the learning process. There are two models that you can use, The PDA Model[46] or The STUMP model, which the PSIA strongly endorses. Both models, can serve as a template on what and how to teach the technical information; however, neither should not restrict you from adding more fun and games to teach the proper body movements for efficient and effective skiing.

The PDA Model[46]

P = Play. Make your lesson fun right from the start. Build team spirit and rapport. They won't remember what you say, but they will remember how you made them feel. This is the time that you initiate the bonding with the child. Ski a run with a game or activity as the focus. This allows you to assess the students and their abilities in a relaxed, nonthreatening atmosphere. The play phase of the lesson should be allotted 15 percent of the time available. They will definitely remember all the fun that they had on the hill.

D = Drills. Base drills on your student's skill development needs. Set up tasks and activities that build skills through play and challenges. Use easy mechanics to remind the student of what they are working on. Set up the child for success (e.g., "Point your toes where you want the skis to go", or "Be Superman/Superwoman and put your hands up for balance control".) The goals should be real and not ideal to meet the student's expectations. Create small goals so that the students will succeed and be encouraged. Do you know what to expect from a performance standpoint with the different age groups? See chapter 8 for realistic goals for each age group.

Keep talk to a minimum. The child has enough on her mind and will probably not hear you anyway. Older students do not want another lecture on the hill. This is not a classroom. Many students already spent four to six hours at their school. They just want to have fun.

The Drill phase of the lesson should be allotted 50 percent of the time available.

Give ample positive feedback and praises to build their self-esteem and confidence.

A = *Adventure*. During this phase, strive for fun through games that will reinforce the skills that are being taught. Be creative and try to find games that are really *fun* to do and ones that they can do. Check for the student's understanding of the skills and tasks taught. Celebrate their accomplishments every opportunity that you have to help build their self-esteem and to motivate them. This phase of the lesson should be allotted to the remaining 35 percent of the time. Watch carefully to make sure that the children understand and enjoy what they are doing. If something is not working, adjust the focus and try again.

STUMP Model[b]

Another approach to creating your lesson plan is by using The STUMP Model·

It is extremely critical that you use the student-instructor-partnership to set the skiing lesson goals, and plan your lesson with flexibility to allow for unexpected conditions. You can all agree on a plan by signing a contract in the snow with your ski poles. Do not set your expectations too high; be realistic. Review the PSIA CAP model, study the snow-texture conditions, and weather conditions. Be mindful of what the child wants. On exceptional days when there is powder or when most of the

---

[b] The following was presented by Sonjia Rom at the New Instructor Training at Boston Mills Ski Resort; Peninsula, Ohio on October 13, 1991.

terrain are a sheet of ice, or when there is constant rain or windy conditions, you may want to alter your plans. Be flexible.

S = State the Goal. For your lesson, the parent and child need to know what you intend to teach. Be concise and clear. Be sure to ask questions if there are any uncertainties.

T = Teach to the Goal. What skills and activities are you going to use to achieve your goal? Be clear, specific, and to-the-point without confusing or frustrating the student. Teach your activities in the proper sequence of progression--simple to the more complex sequence of movements.

U = Check for Understanding. How do you check for understanding? How do you know that they got the message? Do they know Why, How, When, and Where to use that task, skills, and body movements that you just taught?

M = Modify. Sometimes you may have to step back and re-approach the instructions, so that the student can better execute the drill or task. Remember, many times, you can "skin the cat more than one way".

P = Provide a Closure. Tell them how pleased you are with their accomplishments. Communicate with them Why, What, How, Where, they did it so well. Don't sugar-coat your praises, but be truthful and accurate with your comments. Remember to also communicate with their parents; the Parent is the Customer, and the Child is simply the Consumer.

One should be aware of the limitations of the STUMP Model. It can serve as a general template for your lesson plans, but don't let it inhibit your creativity and spontaneity. When coaching children, the instructor needs to be able to teach nonlinearly some of the time. For instance, Ned Pinske says that there are four types of fun that are key to engagement.[36] Playful teaching establishes collaboration, relevancy, a culture of learning, and exploration; it uses four keys that come from video games to create emotional engagement in the learning process. The Four Keys are:

People fun. Collaboration—These activities build social bonds and friendships. It should include play activities that offer both competitive and cooperative opportunities that provides a wide variety of emotional experiences.

Serious fun. Relevancy—These games provide meaning and value to each individual student. For example, personalized purposeful play activities can change how students think, feel, behave, and feel inside.

Hard fun. A culture of learning—These games build a platform that challenge a student but in a form that is achievable in the pursuit of a goal. The focus is on attention and rewards progress to create the alternate emotions, such as frustration and personal triumph.

Easy fun. Exploration—These games offers the novelty of something new and immerse the child in the sheer enjoyment of experiencing the lesson activities. They awaken a sense of curiosity and create intense sensations of wonder, awe, and mystery.

To most of us, happiness focuses on pleasant, positive emotions, and having our needs satisfied. The search for happiness is natural and continuous. Studies have shown that by managing and compiling these four keys of fun, we may actually change our student's brain chemistry.

The bottom line is, create the different kinds of fun. Be involved, excited, and passionate in your role as a teacher/instructor/coach and, always remember, we are in the *fun* business!'

Photo 10. A coach acting as a reindeer to entertain the little children on the beginner hill.

Children are fascinated with magic tricks. They never seem to get enough of this type of entertainment. I spent a whole summer learning this trade.[26, 38] I also purchased books on hand puppets and ventriloquism and practiced these crafts during the off-Winter seasons. Magic tricks, hand puppets, and ventriloquism have help me out of many challenging situations. You may want to give it a try too.

Photo 11. A ski instructor is entertaining children with some magic tricks to create fun and to establish bonding and trust.[16']

Teaching Styles[2-5, 12- 16, 33, 46]

At this juncture, it is important to discuss the teaching styles of a coach. The style used can improve the learning environment of the lesson by enhancing communication and management of the students.

Command. The lesson is controlled fully by the coach, as the child is the center of attention. All explanations, demonstrations, executions and evaluations are made by the instructor. This authoritative style works well with some age groups and not others. This style becomes important when safety instructions and group control become a mandate. Don't be a drill sargent; rather, be a captain of a ship, navigating the crew to paradise.

Guided Discovery. On the other end of the spectrum, the coach simply asks a series of questions and suggests various activities to guide the students to desired results. Keeping that goal in mind, the instructor must skillfully guide children through different tasks to allow them to discover the cause and effect, allowing them to figure out how the task can be accomplished. It is important to realize, the more freedom allowed, the closer monitoring must be employed.

Task. The coach assigns the task and outlines the parameters the students are to use. The child then explains and demonstrates the task, boundaries, and evaluation criteria. The coach moves about, evaluating, encouraging, and giving appropriate feedback.

Reciprocal. The coach establishes a partnership to observe and assess the student's performance. He assigns the students partners so that they can learn from each other. The instructor clearly explains the task, the boundaries, and the evaluation criteria. The coach watches and provides additional constructive feedback to the pair of students. This works best with teens because they do not want to be singled out for fear of losing face in front of their peers.

Problem solving. This approach is like guided discovery; however, the students work on the solutions of a proposed problem, independently or collectively. The coach sets the limits, the boundaries, and time to accomplish the tasks. Be open to the concept that there could be more than one solution to the problem; this teaching style is best used with older children where the cognitive development is more analytical and refined.

Skills Concept and the Five Fundamentals of Skiing Models[46]

Like any sport, skiing requires the development of specific skills. When creating the lesson plan with a goal, you need to be aware of the Skills Concept Model[46], which evolved into the Five Fundamentals of Skiing Model[46] during 2018. This includes (1) direct pressure to the outside ski and pressure control from ski-to-ski, (2) edging control, ankles with inclination and angulation, (3) Keeping the COM over the BOS, (4) control the skis rotation with leg rotation, and (5) regulating the pressure created by ski/snow interaction. As each skill develops, there are common body movements that exhibit themselves in skiers from Level 1 through Level 9 (1, 2, 3 = beginner; 4, 5, 6 = intermediate; 7, 8 = advance; 9 = expert). It is our job as instructors/coaches to evaluate and isolate specific ineffective skills to help our students practice and refine them. Effective movement patterns are often quite different for children than for adults. It is especially important that we exercise patience and use repetition when teaching movements to children. Both the Skills Concept Model and the Five Fundamentals of Skiing[46] compromise the central PSIA philosophy and the American Teaching System. The skills concept categorizes everything we can do that affects going to the right or to the left on a pair of skis. The Five Fundamentals of Skiing Model filters the skills concepts technical framework into what we see as mechanical imperatives for great skiing. Be mindful that The Five Fundamentals of Skiing Model is easier for the child and parent to visualize and comprehend than The Skills Concept Model. I will briefly cover the skills concept model[46] first, rather than The Five Fundamentals of Skiing Model.[46] I will focus on The Five Fundamentals of Skiing and cite references on the skills, which are discussed in greater detail elsewhere in this book. In addition, I will integrate the skill concept model with The Five Fundamentals for Skiing as much as possible. Your challenge as a coach is knowing how to integrate and blend The Skills Concept Model into The Five Fundamentals of Skiing Model.[46]

Skills Concept Model[46]

Edge control. Edge control is the ability to tip the ski onto its edge and adjust the angle between the base of the ski and the snow. The edge angle can be from flat to high, which has a significant impact on speed and directional change. Effective edge control involves using only the amount of edge angle necessary to accurately affect the path of the ski through the arc of the turn. Skiers must move laterally to balance against the forces that act on the skis when they are tipped on edge.

There are two terms commonly used to describe body movements relative to edge-control skills: *angulation* and *inclination*.

Angulation refers to movements that create angles between body parts (e.g., Hip angulation and knee angulation).

Inclination occurs when the skier deviates from a vertical position, which is a general term for any lateral movement toward the inside of the turn brought on by the forces caused during the change in direction of the skis. Other factors that cause inclination include the edge angle used, the turn radius, the pitch of the hill, snow conditions, and speed.

Edge-control skills are discussed further in chapters 3, 6, 8 and 9.

Pressure control. Pressure control requires body movements to manipulate forces, which affect the action of the skis on the snow.

Fore/Aft movements. Pressure can be applied to the entire length of the ski or specific parts of the ski, which requires a forward (Fore) or backward (Aft) adjustment between the skier's center of mass (COM) including the core, and the child's base of support (BOS). The COM is the central balance point of a person's body mass, and the BOS is where the person's weight is distributed on the arches of the feet. A skier may move the COM fore or aft, relative to the BOS by flexing the ankles more (Closing) or, alternately, by pulling both boots back, directly under the COM. Both of these body movements produce the same result by adjusting the pressure fore or aft to attain better balance, so the most effective way to control the fore and aft COM is by flexing and extending the ankles. The ankles are an important part of the movements needed to alter the relationship of the BOS to the COM. *I repeat, the opening and closing of the ankles can move the COM forward and backward relative to the BOS.* In reality, a combination of the ankles, knees, hips, and upper body to are required. The fore/aft pressure along the length of the ski can be controlled by moving the COM, BOS, or a combination of both. Making minute adjustments to these body segments is hard enough as an adult, let alone as a child. Depending on where the young student falls physically in the PSIA CAP Model, these concepts may elude both physically and cognitively. So, the challenge is finding creative ways to get the kids to turn their skis (Rotational control), tip their skis (Edging and pressure control), and direct the pressure along the ski from foot to foot. The challenge is also to manage changes in skis/snow interactions from the bottom of the hill under different snow conditions and steepness.

Another view of pressure control is *releasing* the pressure, instead of pushing, pressing, applying, stepping, flexing, and squashing. Think of it as more like lifting. You can lift your inside knee into your chest, to transfer weight to your outside ski. This method allows you to absorb the energy from rebound (Retraction) and project it in the direction you intend to go. While pulling the inside ski up and back, you lift the outside of the hip and lead with the inside shoulder in (Keeping the strong inside half) to execute super slow, accurate, true parallel turns. When you are comfortable with this sequence of movements, you can increase the pace. These movements are very slight, subtle, deliberate, accurate smooth, like the flow of a great gymnast. You can also lift your toes while creating a well-balanced stance on your foot to allow more closing of the ankles (Dorsal-flex), if needed. More information on pressure control[46]l can be obtained in chapters 3, 6, 8, and 9.

Figure 9. Flamingo drill: lifting one leg and balancing on the other.[46]

Ski-to-ski movements. It is also necessary to control the pressure applied from ski to ski or foot to foot. During the change of direction, pressure applied to the outside ski (Furthest away from the turn), causes the force to push on the skis for the change in direction. When linking the turns, the outside pressure is applied throughout the arc of the turn and then transferred to the new outside ski for the change in direction. This fundamental concept is key to turning. You can mentally picture this by having the old outside leg flex and after finishing the turn to reduce pressure while at the same time the new outside leg extends and lengthens. This extending of the leg increases the pressure on to the new outside ski, thus completing the transfer pressure cycle. In simple kid's terms, it's like riding the bicycle—long leg/short leg. It is important to know that by extending the outside leg, the COM moves across the BOS towards the inside skis and inside the turn. This allows the long leg to create an edge angle and pressure and the short leg to flatten the ski to allow gravity to pull the downhill ski into the turn.

Another approach you can use to teach pressure control is to flex both legs at different rates through the transition from one turn to the next. The old outside leg flexes at a faster rate than the new outside leg. With this method, the COM lowers or remains level with the ground as weight is transferred and the COM and

BOS realign. This can occur in bumps and other variable terrain, and in dynamic short-radius-turn maneuvers.

Pressure control has a unique relationship with *balance*. The skier must maintain equilibrium to stay in balance while adding pressure to bend the skis to allow the change in direction. By adjusting the child's stance to remain in balance during turns, you need to continually make adjustments to increase, decrease, or maintain pressure on the skis. How can you check the child's pressure control? Quite simple: I call it "the gloved hand under the ski" test. Place your gloved hand under the tip region of the ski, have the student apply pressure (Closing the ankles), and check if the child can add varying amounts of pressure onto your gloved hand.

Rotational control. Rotational control refers to turning the skis about the vertical axis of the body. This skill highlights the ability of a skier to control the change in direction of the skis. Be aware of leg rotation and counter-rotation. Leg Rotation is defined as a movement of the lower body to affect the direction the skis point. This includes elements of rotation from the femur in the hip socket and lower-leg or below-the-knee (Ankle) rotation. The upper body should be the anchor (Stable point) for the rotation to be effective. For example, visualize a grandfather clock, the pendulum will not swing properly if the upper portion of the clock is unstable. Thus, keep the upper body stable so the lower body can articulate the movements to affect the skis to change direction. Counter-rotation describes the upper body turns in one direction and the lower body (Hip and legs) turns in the opposite direction. Some call this anticipation, which describes a position or anticipatory movements in preparation for turning. In this case, the upper body actively turns to face downhill rather than across the hill in the direction the skis are pointing. This process is necessary to stretch and engage muscles for the turn. Counter rotation not only provides more edge angles but assists with the turning because the lower body is "twisted" from the upper body and wants to unwind to a neutral position. However, upper-body rotation is typically an inefficient movement in which the upper body turns first, followed by the legs turning in the same direction. Inexperienced skiers tend to use this technique because they do not have the proper body developments or use inappropriate movements because of the lack of knowledge to initiate the turn, (e.g., The child will use the child's upper body to "swing" into the turn). As a coach, you should be aware that depending on the age of the child, they have not developed the upper- and lower-body separation and are more "one-body" in their rotational movements. Why? Because their neuro-musculature development dictates that type of movement. So, for the time being, focus on the lower body by getting the skis to point in the direction of the turns (Rotational skills) until the child has more cognitive and physical developments.

When skiing parallel, both corresponding edges are released simultaneously and both skis are tipped into the turn. The BOS needs to stay under the COS; this is done by pulling the skis slightly back and manage the rebound energy through retraction. When the COS is aligned properly over the BOS, you are in much better dynamic balance. A majority of the skiers push the skis slightly forward; you have just lost balance and power by not being able to flex the ankles enough to pressure the edges. Another issue that contributes to ineffective turn initiation is that skiers lack the patience to let the ski seek the fall line; instead, most skiers push the skis (Heels) laterally to get the skis out of the fall line as quickly as possible, thus interrupting the ability to shape the turn. Great skiers can shape turns in the control phase and are so refined they can adjust the arc of the turn while they are in it by employing DIRT (Duration, intensity, rate, and timing) of the skills applied during the turn. More information on rotational control can be found in chapters 3, 6, 8, and 9.

Balance. What is Balance? Simply put, it is the body's attempt to maintain equilibrium in basically an upright position by conscious and non-conscious (Automatic) reflexes. There are four key body parts that are involved in balance: three sensory organs (Eyes, inner ear, and proprioceptors), and the brain, where incoming information from the three sensors is forwarded to the processing and control center, which is the brain. Proprioception is the body's sense of self-movement and body position. These highly specialized sensory organs send messages to the brain about the limb's velocity and movements, the amount of load on a limb, and the limb limits. These complex series of neuromuscular networks account for knowing where our body parts are in the environment and helping maintain a desired position. See photograph 5, showing a young child on the balance beam. Knowing this, what can you do to improve the child's balance? See photographs 13 and 15 for a good athletic stance for a child. Practice, practice, practice the right fundamental movements. All athletes practice fundamental movements intensely with the guidance of a skilled coach. As in golf, my coach once told me, "Practice is useless if you don't practice the proper skills and mechanics of the golf swing. If you don't, when you go to the practice range, all that you will do is just reinforce bad habits."

Photo 12. Coaches and students working on balance and weight transfer by lifting one foot off the ground while transferring the body weight to the other foot while trying to maintain balance.[46]

How can we translate the physiological definition of balance into a practical and realistic definition? Since the majority of an instructor's focus in working on balance during various activities. In this discussion, I will utilize the five fundamentals of skiing (Which is discussed extensively in the next section in this chapter)[46] to illustrate the movements necessary for turning. In a static exercise, Balance begins with the lower body; the center of mass (COM) should be balanced over the arch of the foot (The base of support, BOS) by flexing the ankles to get the knees move forward (Passed the toes). Flex at the hips so the upper torso is bent parallel to the lower leg (tibia and fibula) with the arms and hands forward. For aggressive skiing the balance point of the BOS shifts forward—more towards the balls of the foot, depending on how aggressive one is skiing and other conditions. Most skiers have not mastered the athletic stance when we tell them to **"stand like an athlete,"** but most students don't master it. I have a perfect stick model that may help (See figure 10.) Since we spend the majority of our time teaching turning maneuvers of different shapes, size, and speed, let us focus on balance as we go through the turn.

There are four phases of the Turn: (1) Phase 0, or transition phase, (2) Phase 1, or turn initiation, (3) Phase 2, or shaping of the turn, and (4) Phase 3, or Finishing of the Turn.

Figure 10. A stick model of a perfect athlete stance. Then ankles, knees, and hip simultaneously flex so the COM moves forward. Notice that the 30-degree bend of the upper torso and upper leg (Including the core) matches to the flex of the lower leg (Is parallel). To be in the balance position, the COM must be centered over the BOS (Over the arch of each foot).

Four Phases of the Turn: There are *four phases of the turn:* (1) Phase 0 or *Transition Phase, which is not usually mentioned in the PSIA manual,* (2) Phase 1 or *Turn initiation,* (3) Phase 2 or *Shaping of the Turn.* And (4) Phase 3 or *Finishing of the turn.*

Photo 13. A three-year-old girl is in a good athletic stance.[5] Note: her ankles are flexed to move the COM forward to be centered on her feet (BOS).[46]

Photo 14. A young girl with too wide a wedge, which causes her to sit back (COM falls behind the BOS); this results her to compromise her athletic stance[5] and be out of balance.[46]

Transition phase. While this is an often times neglected discussion, this is an important phase of the turn. Many skiers are out of balance as they finish a turn and enter this regrouping phase. If one is out of alignment and balance, there are couple of things one can accomplish to re-center the COM over the BOS during this phase.

One is flexing (Closing) the ankles to get the COM to move forward, and second is to pull both feet (BOS) back under the COM. Most skiers tend to rush going from one turn to the next without giving *themselves enough time to regroup. One of the drills that I have the students do is the 2-4-2 edging concept.* Give sufficient amount of time when the student has four edges on the snow to allow time to get back into balance so that one can begin the turn initiation more effectively with edges engaged from both skis.

Turn initiation. The beginner skier in the wedge platform can begin to initiate the turn by moving the COM diagonally towards the inside (Downhill) skis tip. This causes the outside (Uphill) leg to lengthen and the inside (Downhill) leg to actively retract—like pedaling the bicycle (e.g., Pushing down on one pedal as the other pedal moves up) or doing heavy foot/light foot. The skis will react by the outside ski having more edge angle and pressure to initiate a change in direction of the ski. The inside leg is actively shortened and is thereby closer to the center of the body with little or no edge angle (Almost flattened on the snow). This causes the ski to release the contralateral edge to disengage from the snow and allow gravity to pull the inside tip downhill as the uphill or outside ski follows. The movements for the parallel skier follow the same sequence of events, except that both corresponding edges engage the snow at relatively the same time and causes both skis to change direction in unison. With both the wedge and parallel skier, the rotary skill is also used to blend with the edging and pressure skill to start the turn. It is key to remember that weight transfer shifts from a neutral position to the outside ski and one should be balanced throughout the turn on that one ski.

Shaping of the turn. This is the fastest phase of the turn because of the amount of time spent in the fall line. The greatest speed and force occur at the apex of the arc. The speed is determined by the turn shape (See figure 12) and by the size of the wedge (See figure 14), and whether one is using a wedge or parallel platform (See figure 17). The shape, size, and speed of the turn are determined by **DIRT** (Duration of the turn, Intensity of the pressure, Rate of the turn, Timing of the turns).

Photo 15. An eight-year-old girl demonstrating good five fundamentals of skiing[29]. Notice the flexing of the ankles to get the COM forward with the arms, hands, and poles forward. This athletic stance[5, 46] allows her to use her rotary-, edging- and pressure-control skills with ease to make the turns.

Finishing the turn. The major objective of the finishing phase of the turn is to control one's speed. Many students do not finish their turns and they tend to pick up too much speed and get out of balance and control. Coaches should emphasize the importance of this phase of the turn.

Photo 16. A ten-year-old boy drops his arms, hands, and poles after finishing a turn. This causes him to be out of balance because his COM is now behind his BOS.[46]

Other considerations on balance. A common debate is whether being in a state of dynamic balance creates the ability to move more effectively by using the other three skills, or vice versa. The answer for this dual role of balance is yes. In addition, you need to recognize the interdependent relationship between the skills and balance, the results of effective and efficient movements. Since the majority of your students are out of balance (Usually in the "back seat," of the middle of the skis), focus your attention on this movement skill. The size of a younger child's head is larger in proportion to their body. When coupled with growing motor-skill developments, the aforementioned can change the balance points. Because PSIA and AASI have made gradual modifications over the years by *not* considering balance as a skill but rather an outcome of developing the blended elements (Skills) of the edge control, pressure control, and rotary control, examine how we use these elements in the five fundamentals of skiing throughout the text. More discussion on balancing skills can be found in chapters 3, 6, 8, and 9.

Five Fundamentals of Skiing Model[46]

This section will provide you with a short overview of this important model. Additional readings are provided in the references. You should always be aware that there are important relationships of structure and fun[46] as they relate to the needs of the parent and child (See figure 11). All too often, I have observed that the ski lesson is designed with too much structure and information and not enough fun, or vice versa. And I have seen customer satisfaction not being met because of the idealistic goals of both the parent and child exceeded the realistic goals. The crossover point in the graft is on a sliding scale (e.g., A young toddler wants more fun and less structure and information, while the older student needs more structure and information and a little less playing). Achieving the crossover point for both the parent and child where there is a happy medium between structure and fun is a constant moving target. Communication is key, and understanding the PSIA CAP model and being creative are essentials for developing a successful lesson plan for both your customers.

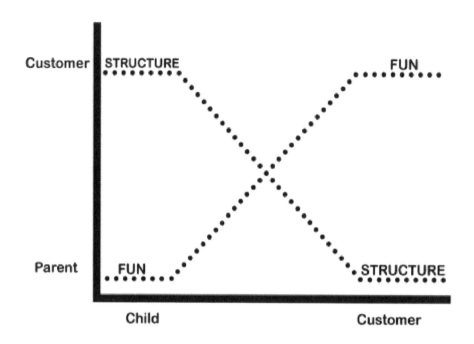

Figure 11. Modified drawing on the interrelationship of structure and fun and what the parent and child require[46]

Direct pressure to the outside ski and pressure control from ski to ski. Transferring your weight to the outside or inside ski while remaining balanced is not an easy feat. It is fundamental goal to get balanced over the downhill or outside ski or balanced over the uphill or inside ski. When making a right turn, it is a left-footed turn; and when making a left turn, it is a right-footed turn. Pressure increase/decrease can be achieved multiple of ways, one of which is by lengthening the leg and another by shortening the leg. The ankles (Opening and closing) and the knees both play a major role in extension and flexing motion. Retraction of the legs is another way of adjusting the pressure on the skis. Drills that can be utilized for this fundamental skill is discussed further in chapters 3, 6, 8, and 9.

Photo 17. A four-year-old girl is scooting around on her 'scooter' to practice weight transfer for pressure and balance control on the one 'scooter' while maintaining balance.[46]

Photo 18. A twelve-year-old boy is using the Five Fundamentals of Skiing[46] when making a left turn. Notice: he transfers his weight to the right ski and extends his right leg to create increasing pressure and edge angle and having the left ski flattening out by retracting the left leg.

Photo 19. Even a four-year-old girl, like the eleven-year-old boy in photo 18, can make great turns using the Five Fundamentals of Skiing[46] if the ski instructor coaches a student properly.

Control edge angles with inclination and angulation. Tipping the skis on to their edges involves inclining the body toward the inside of the turn in the direction you are turning; it also involves angulating the upper body back toward the skis (Toward the outside of the turn). When making a right turn and traversing the hill, move the uphill hip and shoulder up; keep the downhill hip and shoulder down. The opposite movements are done with a left turn. The COS needs to move in the direction of the turn. As discussed in the Skills Concept Model, edging can be achieved through inclination, angulation, or both. The foot or ankle articulation also plays a role in edging. Drills for this fundamental skill are discussed further in chapter 3, 6, 8, and 9.

Keeping the COM over the BOS. Controlling the COM to stay over the BOS is always a challenge during any type of skiing. Staying in balance to utilize the entire length of the skis, the front of the skis, and the back of the skis, when need, is a tough fundamental to master. The results of this control are better stability and balance and better control on how the skis turn. Staying in balance in the center of the skis is your primary goal. See drills in chapters 6 and 9 for more edging activities. This concept of attaining dynamic balance is covered extensively throughout this manual. See "Movement Analysis" in this chapter and "Balancing Drills" in chapter 3, 6, 8, and 9.

Photo 20. This three-year-old boy is skiing out of balance;[46] the cues[16] are his left ski is on an inside edge and the body is tilting to the right, causing lateral imbalance[46']

Controlling the skis' rotation. This can be achieved by turning, pivoting, or steering with leg rotation that is separate from the upper body. The upper body (Core) should be quiet and stable, while the lower body rotates independently by twisting the femur (Upper leg) in the hip socket to the right or to the left. More is covered above in the skills concept model section under "Rotational Control" and in chapters 6, 8, and 9.

Regulate the magnitude of pressure created through ski/snow interactions. You can create resistance by pushing down on the snow. The force a ski puts into the snow acts at a right angle to its surface. The reaction force also acts at a right angle to the base of the ski. There are two things that you can do with a ski that will affect the reaction force and its components. The first is to tilt a ski onto its edge, and the second is to change the angle that a ski is pointing in, along its length. As a ski's resistance comes from the ski's reaction from the snow, two forces can push the ski into the snow: gravity and a momentum-induced force from changing your velocity. Gravity always acts straight downwards, with a set force. The momentum-induced force will only act if you are changing velocity; this creates a G-force as we turn. This is a difficult topic to understand, but whenever you go out skiing, focus on the forces that create pressure. Try to determine how the pressure skills are interwoven into the Five Fundamentals of Skiing Model[46].

    1) When contemplating an activity, ask yourself these questions:

    2) What movement pattern will we be practicing?

    3) Why are we going to perform this activity?

    4) How will it enhance my lesson and affect our skiing today?

    5) Where are we going to do the drills?

Movement Analysis[2,3,16,17,33,46]

A large part of being a successful and outstanding kid's coach is the evaluation of effective versus ineffective movements. Most of the evaluation deals with movement analysis, or simply put, describing movements and understanding their relevance.

To help a student improve, first compare their current level of performance with the desired new level:

A. Define the Challenge:

- What is the current situation and why is this a challenge?
- What would it take to resolve the challenge?
- What is the outcome? Did the drills and new body movements resolve the challenge? How do you know?
- What are the obstacles to solving the challenge? Were you able to circumvent them and achieve your goals?
- Where do the students want to go? What are their goals?
- Where are they now with their goals?
- What will it take to get to the new performance level?
- Do not concentrate on what your expectations and goals are, but instead, replace it with what the student thinks is "good". If the student is seeking something that is functionally in error, you will be better able to help them correct the misconceptions

B. Solve the Challenge:

- What can you first do to solve the challenges?

- Try it. Did it work?
- If it didn't work, do you have stepping-stones[16] to other pathways that resolve the challenge?

Always be aware that a lesson is fluid by nature and circumstances can change as learning proceeds. Do not get locked in or into a rigid idea of what is good. Be flexible.

Only by analyzing the student's actual performance on the snow will you know what the overall picture looks like. What are the skis doing on the snow? How are the body parts moving? What's the PSIA CAP developmental stage of the child? It is only by answering these questions that you can formulate the correct prescription for change to help the student achieve their goals. Here are some of the major challenges that I have experienced with the different age groups:

Always begin by analyzing what the skis are doing. Then work your way up to examine what the ankles, knees, hips and upper torso are doing, which might give you a clue how they might be affecting the skis. If you want a deeper understanding of the mechanics of skiing, some of you may want to delve into the physics of skiing[5].

Take a first-impression snapshot of your student. What strikes you and what is the major cause of the challenge? There may be many causes for the effects that you are observing. You may want to go for the biggest bang for the money by first working on the skill that will have a major impact in improving the major problem or challenge.

The major challenges for the three- to six-year old:

- walking around in their heavy boots
- maneuvering their heavy and cumbersome skis around on flat land
- achieving the correct athletic stance[7]
- being balanced on the moving skis[46]
- making directional changes
- learning how to get up
- climbing the hill (Side-steps, herringbone steps)
- controlling their speed down the hill

The major challenges for the seven- to ten-year old:

- achieving the proper athletic stance[5] at all times
- fear of the steeper hills
- learning the fundamental movements of turning
- controlling their speed
- learning to get up on steeper terrain
- climbing the hill by themselves

The major challenges for the eigh-year old and older students:

- achieving the correct athletic stance[7] throughout the entire turn
- fear of the steeps and jumps
- not finishing their C-turns
- not understanding the consequences of bombing the hill at mach-2 speeds
- making unnecessary foolish and risky stunts that compromise the safety of others and themselves
- can get bored easily or can't wait to show off to the opposite gender or to other people on the slopes
- needs further refinement of the fundamentals of turning

Narrow the focus and prioritize what you see that needs major and immediate improvements:

- Balance and stance? One of the major challenges for all age groups is maintaining balance ("Knees ahead of the toes, nose ahead of the toes, and hands up and ahead of the knees"). A great drill to do for homework is pretending to be a flamingo; see how long they can lift the one leg. Make it fun by the parents timing their child to see which leg is stronger and more neuro-muscularly coordinated (See figure 9). I also ask the child, "does your parent drive the car in the back seat or front seat?" They'll usually say, front seat! Then I'll say, "well, you're driving those skis; you better be in the front seat!"

- Turn entry? Check to see when and where the child is doing the turn iniation.

- Turn shape? Examine what size and shape are turns; are they "Z-" or "C-" shaped?
- Loss of speed control? Is the child in control of his/her speed?

When analyzing the problems, start with an understanding of cause and effect. Look for cues[17]; always, always start from the bottom (i.e. What are the skis doing? and work your way up (What are the body parts doing?). For example, for CAUSE, what are ankles, knees, hips, upper torso (Including the core), head, arms, hands doing? They will give you cues on the effects on the skis. When you observe ineffective cues, what phase of the turn is it occurring (See in this chapter under "Balance")?. Always have a potential solution by reverting to the Five Fundamentals of Skiing[46] to correct the problem(s).

Here are some examples:

Cause: Being out of balance.

Effect: The COM has shifted laterally from the BOS.

Solution: The skier needs to realign himself/herself to be centered over the skis for a better Athletic Stance5.

Photo 21: This young lad is out of alignment causing his COM to shift onto his left ski as his right ski raises off the snow..[17, 46] –

Cause: not enough edge angle or pressure, or both.

Effect: the skis are skidding during the turns.

Solution: work on creating more edge angles with specific drills (See chapter 6 and photos 18, 50, and 52).

Cause: the upper body is tipped to the inside of the finishing phase of the turn.

Effect: the skier loses the ability to apply pressure to the outside ski.

Solution: work on proper timing of weight transfer and proper body alignment over the BOS.

Cause: the inside ski has too much edge angle or too much edge pressure, or a combination of both.

Effect: the inside ski turns sooner than the outside ski, resulting in the tips to separate and form a Y-shape during the turn?

Solution: work on proper weight distribution on each ski, equal edge angle on both skis, equal amount of pressure on each ski, and proper stance. Focus on the COM being centered over the BOS.

Cause: too much pressure is applied to the inside ski, resulting in the inside ski bending more than the outside ski[46].

Effect: inside ski will turn sooner than the outside ski, causing the ski tips to deviate.

Solution: work on creating proper edge angle and pressure distribution throughout the turn to get both skis to move together to obtain equal distance between both skis (See photo 97 and 50).

Cause: skier is not fluid, but stiff throughout the turns.

Effect: the static or stiff skier gets bounced bound around by the terrain, causing the skier to be out of balance.

Solution: determine the cause of the rigid profile; if it is anxiety or fear, or too-rigid stance, work on the underlying problem.

Cause: the skier is tipping the skis too early in the turn

70

Effect: this can create a fast and heavy edge set at the end of the turn, creating Z-Turns and not C-Turns.

Solution: work on being in balance before, during, and finishing the turn. Inform the student that they need to be patient during the shaping phase of the turn; one can count numbers through each phase of the turn.

Cause: the skier's movements into the turns are ineffective, causing a loss of alignment and balance.

Effect: the turns are not smooth and consistent from turn to turn.

Solution: work on a single turn with the proper sequence of progressive movements. Once this is mastered on a lower terrain, work on linking the turns with the focus on smoothness and with proper turn shape and size consistency.

Cause: the skier moves the child's COM backward instead of in a diagonal direction towards the new turn.

Effect: the skier is no longer in balance to allow the other skills to work.

Solution: work on the athletic stance5 throughout the turn on a lower grade hill. Drills such as shuffle turns, hop turns, one thousand steps will be helpful (See chapter 6 and photo 13).

Cause: some of the skier's joints flex too much and others not enough throughout the turns.

Effect: edging control, pressure control, rotary control may be compromised, which may cause the skier to be out of balance.

Solution: first start with static drills (Shin-Tung exercises, rocking fore/aft in the boot, jumping), followed by dynamic drills (Picking apples, jump shots with a basketball, side slip, falling leaf). See chapter 6 for drills.

Cause: the skier's shoulders and/or upper body initiate the turning of the skis.

Effect: the skier is not allowing the upper body to be quiet and stable to allow the lower body to move the skis in the intended direction.

Solution: work on the upper body to be stable and lower body movements to allow the skis to make the turns. Focus on achieving more edge and pressure control, drills with steering, and drills with static and dynamic balance (See chapter 6).

Cause: the skier's hands and hips are behind the child's feet.

Effect: the skier to be out of alignment with the COM falling behind the BOS leading to imbalance. (See photo 16).

Solution: focus on creating a better stance. Work on flexing/extension of the ankle so that the knees, hips, hands and nose are in the forward position. Bending your back from the hip helps to attain an athletic stance.

Cause: the pole touches are incorrectly positioned or the timing of the turns become erratic.

Effect: the turns are not smooth and consistent.

Solution: teach the proper use of the poles (See chapter 9).

Cause: the skier is looking at the tips of the skis.

Effect: the skier is looking down, causing him/her to be out of the athletic stance.

Solution: pick a target so the child can look towards the designated target when skiing. Ask him/her what color, shape, image it was to check if that target was really looked at.

All of these examples could influence the quality of your student's skiing. Like a good doctor, coaches cannot fix the problem without the proper diagnosis. Proper treatment can only be prescribed if the coach's observations are accurate. So, as a coach, you need to train your eyes and brain to make the movement analysis a reality and be able to provide accurate solutions to fix the ineffective cues.

The Learning Partnership[16, 33, 46]

An integral part of teaching is knowing the learning partnership. It can best be understood knowing the personal profile, motivations, knowledge, and experiences of both the coaches and students bring to the learning environment.

Student's Profile[16, 33, 46,]

The student's profile covers a wide range of characteristics that make a person unique i.e. shaping their behavior and affecting their capacity to learn, as well as their emotional and physical developments. Other factors, such as educational background, number of extracurricular activities that they participated in, and other life experiences and genetic factors also play a role on their learning and performance on the snow. Their past experiences, identity, values, beliefs, attitudes and emotional states, goals and motivation, drive, physical condition and health, and learning style will make up the composition of the student's profile. I always try to ask, "What's your favorite sport, hobby, educational subject, pet, movie?" to obtain a student's profile from the child's own perspective. See chapter 1 on capitalizing on horse riding training knowledge and teaching skiing.

Instructor's Profile[16, 33, 46]

Likewise, be sure that your customers know who you are. The instructor's profile includes the acquired technical knowledge to teach skiing, performance level, motivation to coach well, confidence, creativity and imagination to teach the progression of movements, skills, and mechanics to effectively change performances to the desired outcomes, *and* something personal about yourself. During the introduction phase, don't just stop at saying, "Hi, I'm your coach, Brad."

Without much background provided, your customer may have a difficult time remembering you. They will often say, "Yeah, I had this terrific coach, but I can't remember his name!" How, are you going to get repeat customers or referrals? Use a business card, or use a catchy name which will stick. Over the initial years, I got tired of students and parents forgetting my name, so I came up with "Pineapple Herb" and it stuck, whether I was at Boston Mills, Brandywine, Alpine Valley, or Deer Valley Ski Resorts. It also gave me a ticket to be an entertainer about Hawaii. On the chair lift, I would ask them, "What part of the pineapple is the sweetest?", or "How long does it take to ripen before you can eat it?", or "It is eighty degrees in Honolulu today". "Do we have snow on the islands?", or "What does *wiki wiki* (Hurry up), *mahalo* (Thank you), *pupule* (Crazy person), *ono* (Delicious), *wahine* (Women or girl), *kane* (Men or boy), *kapuu* (Save or reserve) mean in English?"

I remembered on one sunny day, I ran out to greet a group of beginners and said, "The front desk informed me that the surf is up. Who wants to learn surfing?" What a response I got! My point is, be creative and unique! Create an identity of your own so you will always be remembered. For example, you can tell them how you milked your first goat or rattlesnake or rode an elephant or camel or went down in a shark-protection cage or held a twenty-foot anaconda or went sky diving or rode in a B-17 bomber! You can even tell them about your first experience trying to hit that tiny white ball with a stick with a small club head. Many call this sport golfing. I call it flogging (Golf spelled backwards)! Teaching skiing is unique at every resort. As a professional, your understanding and awareness of the various services provided at your resort adds tremendous value to your guests. You need to be current with all school programs, fees, policies and procedures, lodging accommodations, terrain, hazardous mountain areas, snow conditions, and weather. But, I recapitulate, one of the most important traits to focus and develop is *creativity*.

Time Management[27]

One final neglected consideration when developing your lesson plan is *time management*. If you want to observe a parent's hair turning grey just before your eyes, deliver their child late or lose your kid! They are already anxiety ridden because their precious child is out there trying to survive the weather, the terrain, and everything one could possibly fathom. There are many things that you need to consider:

Do you have a watch on your uniform (Jacket) so you can quickly glance at it without being obvious?

Do you know the time it takes to the top of a chairlift at the different locations on the hill? Knowing these times can assist you with being on time.

Do you know how long it takes to get down from the top of a chairlift after allowing for buffers (e.g., Missing a direction, falling group of kids and equipment on a steep hill, having to make a pitstop at the mid-lodge, taking the time out after the child had a slight accident) when going back to a destination like the ski lodge? This is part of time management.

Do you have the necessary telephone numbers if you do get delayed? A good practice is to exchange telephone number with your student's parents, ski Patrol, front desk, and so on. Be sure to consult with management for the appropriate protocol at your ski resort.

Do you know precisely where and to whom you need to deliver that child? Usually there is a common returning point at the resort, but sometimes, the parents want to meet their child at another location.

Do you know exactly what time the parents are expecting you (It is not uncommon for the parents to alter the lesson plans and want their child delivered earlier or at a different location)?

Be conscientious about time management! It is a serious commitment to good customer service. If you make too many such mistakes, especially if you lose their kid, be sure to carry a carton of hair-coloring kit as a gift for their worrying parent with the newly formed gray hairs!

Distractions[27]

Every attempt should be made to minimize distractions. For instance, in a private lesson, minimize your greetings and discussions to other fellow ski instructors, other guests, and management when you are walking out with your clients; your students are paying for this lost time. Do not answer incoming telephone calls; turn the ringer off! There are limited times that you can use the mobile phone; that is for the use of the camera. Most people like photographs of themselves on the slopes doing beautiful ski turns or just want the beautiful scenery with them in the picture. If you do, ask permission to take any pictures of your students. Use the pictures for absolutely nothing else except for their purpose. All photographs are protected by copyright laws. If you do want to use the photos of your students for other purposes, you need the parent's and their child's written permission, by signing a photograph release form. One final topic about distractions; try to cut the useless chatter while riding on the chairlifts; have meaningful conversations that will motivate children, increase the learning process or provide entertainment for building trust or bonding.

Etiquette/People Skills[27]

Be chivalrous at all times. When your client or other guests are entering or leaving the lodge or bathroom, open the door or hold the door open for them. If they are carrying their skis to the rack, carry it for them if they seem to be struggling. Demonstrate your client -service skills and offer assistance to customers who want their pictures taken on the premise; any attempt to be super creative to go the extra mile for them. If they looked confused, assist them with directions or any other questions that they may have. If they need help with their equipment (Ski breaks, helmet, goggles), be of service to them. How many times have you seen a person struggling to get the pair of skis untangled because the ski brakes are hindering the release of each ski? Did you make a special effort to assist that individual even though you were in the middle of having your lunch? Inform your students that when they are in the chairlift line to allow enough space between them and the person ahead of them by not touching or bumping their skis. If the food court is crowded, give up your seat for them. These are all your customers; a little bit of consideration and thoughtfulness goes a long way!

Fully understanding what causes the skis to move the way they do through accurate movement analysis will assist you with correcting the problems associated with ineffective and inefficient skiing. In addition, know how to blend the Skills Concept Model into the Five Fundamentals of Skiing with authority. Don't be too wordy with your presentations; *be brief, be brilliant be gone!* Acknowledge the importance of proper time management, etiquette, and knowing how to limit your distractions from your clients and your lessons.

CHAPTER 4

Developing a Strong Foundation—
Building Safety into your Coaching

As we stated in chapter 1, to bond with the parent and child, you need to promise them that *safety* is highest on your coaching agenda. There are more than three hundred million snow sport enthusiasts throughout the world, and accidents do happen. It is estimated that over six hundred thousand injuries are reported each year nationally as a result of skiing and snowboarding. Make sure that you fully understand your ski resort's safety policy. Indicate how you intend to implement this into your lesson plans. Later, at the closing, explain to the parent and child how and where you taught *safety*.

Every ski resort has their version of the responsibility code[2-5, 12-14, 33, 46, 47]

A = Above: Always be visible to skiers above you.

B = Breaks: Be sure to have brakes working and retention strap on your skis poles to prevent runaway equipment.

C = Control: Be sure you ski in control at all times.

D = Downhill: The downhill skier has the right-of-way.

E = Enter: Enter trails safely—whenever starting downhill or merging on a new trail, always look uphill and yield.

F = Follow: Follow all posted signs, stay off of closed trails.

G = Get: Get on and off the chairlifts safely. Know how to load, ride and unload the chair properly and safely.

If you want to cut to the chase and simplify your Safety presentation, try using my modified version of what Deer Valley Ski Resort uses;[52] I modified it to DUCKS'S:

D = Downhill skier has the right-of-way.

U = Always look Up Hill before pulling out.

C = Always ski in Control.

K = Know and follow all the rules and posted signs.

S = Stop where you can be visible from above.

S = Safely load, ride, and unload the people mover conveyer belt and chairlift.

How do you check for understanding the safety rules that you have just taught? Don't assume your verbal instructions will stick or make sense. You need to find ways to verify what they really understand and how completely they understand the safety rules under different circumstances. For instance, try role-playing and switching roles. You become the student and the student becomes the coach. So, I ask the young coach, "I'm looking above me for oncoming traffic and the traffic below seems clear. Can I go down the hill now?" If the answer is correct, I praise them for their excellence. I also tell their parents about each role-played for safety and how it went. If the answer is not correct, then I explain the ramifications of the wrong decisions and provide a better alternative.

I use another method to check the understanding of safety; I use reality checks for safety. I ask the student, "Who's your best friend? OK, the child is waiting for you down at the bottom of the hill, and you decide to bomb the hill at high speed to show off and you smack him, which results in a fractured leg in three places. The child is in a cast and on crutches for the rest of the spring through fall. The child misses his family vacation to Paris, France."

Then, I ask the student, "How do you really feel about that?"

I then reverse the person; the student is now waiting at the bottom of the hill waiting for his best friend to come down. The child's best friend cannot control the speed and is out of control. Not being able to turn, he hits the student, and the child is in a coma for four weeks. I said, "The child remains in the hospital for multiple tests and has to do weeks of physical therapy. The sad thing is the child cannot go to the child's summer camp, which is always a sought-after annual event with friends." I ask the victim, "How do you really feel about that mishap?"

Usually, the answers are not good or pleasant. Reality and realization will set in and can make a big difference on how kids behave and how they perceive the importance of safety. The reasoning and wisdom centers in the brain's frontal lobe does not fully mature until a person is twenty-five years old. Kids are susceptible to wrong decisions. I suspect that in some adults who are skiing on the slopes recklessly, the center for wisdom, logic, and common sense never fully matured!

If your student does fall or get into an accident, show lots of empathy, concern, and love. Don't be afraid to give lots of fist bumps, high-fives, ski-pole taps, or verbal praises when they get up. I tell them that, "We all fall, but the main thing is to be able to get up by yourself and persevere on to the next venture. Better yet, try to understand what caused your fall and try not to repeat that mistake."

People-mover or conveyer-belt systems are technological developments that assist the students in getting up the beginner hill conveniently and effortlessly. They come in different lengths and configurations. I have seen my share of accidents on these devices and would like to spend some time on how to prevent accidents. We probably have one of the steepest beginner slopes in the country; perhaps that is why it seems that we have more mishaps than we should. Accidents appear to be more likely when we have ice storms and high winds. I have observed kids falling down while on a moving conveyer belt and receiving lacerations and mild concussions. I have even seen adults falling and ended up twisting both legs that led to a sprained ankle or pulled muscle. Our resort does not have the luxury of having lift-operator attendants to assist customers on and off the belt. So, these devices are not seemingly accident-free. I will first instruct my little munchkin to first change the child's pizza shape to French fries as the child approaches the conveyer Belt. Then, I shuffle forward to the moving belt, being aware that he/she needs to be prepared for the tug when getting on the moving belt. I will assist the child by holding the child's hand to guide the child onto the moving carpet. As soon as my client is on, I will immediately hop on with both ski poles in one hand, directly behind her. I will move up and snuggle up to the child, all the while holding her safely up to the top. During the viral pandemic I needed to adjust my approach by being six-feet behind the customer. If the child struggles unloading (Because of snow accumulating at the top of the conveyer belt), I will use both handle end of the of the ski poles to push him/her forward off the carpet. We will both quickly move away to prevent congestion in that area. Then we will both move away from the area, avoiding being close to the conveyer belt. I have observed children sliding under the carpet when there was no protection cover. Consider the people-mover safety protocol with your utmost attention. The last thing that you want is to report to the child's parent that you had an accident with their kid!

Photo 22. A four-year-old girl being assisted by a ski instructor to load onto the Conveyer Belt for safety reasons.

Carpet squares. An alternative method of going up the hill is using strips of carpets or 2' x 2' carpet squares that you can line up the hill. The length up the hill can be adjusted by the number of squares that you use. This adjustability has the advantage over the Conveyer Belt, which may go too far up the hill for some beginning students.

Photo 23. Young kids climbing the beginner hill on a temporary, length-adjustable carpet for safety reasons

Chairlifts need special attention because of the many horrific stories we have all read in the newspapers and magazines. According to the National Ski Areas Association (NSSA), 88 percent of the accidents are on the hill, 5 percent in the terrain park, and 4 percent from falls from the chairlifts. Most of the chairlift accidents occur with ages ten or under. According to NSSA, there are 3,500 chairlifts in the USA, and 90 percent of the accidents are due to human error. Most of the lifts are either quads or triple chairlifts, and riding them requires special attention[45]. The skis and boots of a child are proportionally greater in weight as compared to the rest of the body; thus, sliding under the safety bar is more common than you think. Children are especially vulnerable when the seats are wet or icy. If you are riding up with one child, load the child on the lift operator's side. Or, when you are lucky enough to have another adult to ride with you, place the child in the center, as seen in photos 24 and 25. If you have more than one child on a triple chair, the instructor should sit in the middle, and each child should sit all the way back and hold onto the armrest. If you have a group lesson, have a willing guest ride up with the same seating arrangement to load the rest of your class. On a quad chair, use the same arrangement; never put two kids together to fill the space because the paired kids will without a doubt play. For older kids, have each kid be sit on each end of the triple or quad chair only if you know for certain that they are mature enough to follow instructions. Demonstrate responsible behavior by sitting back, keeping still, having each child holding the outside handrails, looking ahead, and instructing them to never clap their skis together to remove the snow, least the skis will come off and hit someone below. I have personally witnessed a child's ski coming off and hitting someone below, causing a skull fracture. Always be sure that the safety bar is down; if they need assistance, be sure to inform the lift operator.

Another issue that needs attention is a child using their poles to load or unload, which may interfere with their partner coming on or off the lift; always instruct the student tha the/she to carry both poles in one hand with the pole tips high off the ground during loading and unloading of the chair. If the child does fall after unloading, educate the child to quickly get up and move out of the way for safety reasons. If they cannot get up, at least try to crawl out of the way or holler to the lift attendant at the top to stop the chairlift. When getting off the chairlift, inform your student that they need to prevent congestion in the area; move away quickly so that others can come off the chair safely and go to their desired location to go down the hill.

Demonstrate proper etiquette when standing in the lift line; inform your student to not let their skis move ahead and hit the person's skis in front of them. They might get annoyed because they spent a lot of money on their precious skis. As a stewart of good moral judgment, teach your student to always have their moral compass pointing to true north at all times!

How many times have you seen a tiny child not being able to get on or off the chair? It is particularly difficult when a child's buttock does not reach the chair and the chairlift hits them and they fall down; they try to get up, and the child gets hit in the head by the oncoming chair. It is the same with unloading: when the child cannot reach the landing platform, the child will attempt to jump off the chair. Therefore, pay particular attention to a child's height relative to the chair's height. Make a sound judgement before you the munchkins up the chairlift. During both the loading and unloading process, it is your responsibility to carry the child using whatever technique works for you. In addition, don't be afraid to tell the lift operator to slow down the chairlift to assist you and the student. During the loading process, the child may need some help going from the first red line (Waiting line) to the second red line (Loading line). When the student is on the chair, be sure the child scoots all the way to the back of the chair and hold on to the armrest. On the ride up, the student should look forward and not wiggle around or play. For added security, I will usually put my arms around their shoulders and hold them. If you'll need help with the unloading process, have the lift operator at the bottom to phone up to the operator at the top to slow the chairlift down so you can do your unloading safely.

Photo 24. When a child's buttock is below the chair, they will need assistance to get up on the chairlift, especially when it moves at a high speed.

Photo 25. Two coaches safely unloading a three-year-old girl off the chairlift for the first time and helping her down a steep ramp.

In addition, there are other safety guidelines that need special attention with COVID-19. With the viral air-borne pandemic, the ski industry is going through a major revolution for safety.[25] In conjunction with the National Ski Areas Association (NSAA) and PSIA/AASI encourages everyone to follow the national guidelines, "Ski Well, Be Well" (nsaa.org/skiwellbewell). Review periodic guidelines for safety updates that are aligned with the Centers for Disease Control (tiny.cc@COVID-19CDCGuidelines). This is your responsibility! All ski resorts all over the world are struggling to maintain pandemic safety and have posted many rules for protection; the past two years have been of experimentation for survival.[c] There are other ways that you can help protect yourself from this virus,[39] besides distancing yourself, wearing a facial mask or balaclava, and sanitizing your hands and ski gloves often. There is absolutely no doubt that wearing a mask and social distancing are wordy protection for the pandemic. However, I have discovered that there are at least three compromises when you are coaching. (1) You will have difficulty communicating; your students cannot hear you and you cannot hear them. The mask will act like a car muffler to reduce the engine noise. So, at the very beginning of the lesson, you need to carefully explain that you will try to speak *louder* and more *clearly*; if they cannot hear you, inform them that they should say, "Please repeat that coach." You may want to step back and temporarily lift your mask from your lip and let the volume of air and sound to more readily reach your student(s). The student can do the same thing so that you can also hear them. I can't imagine the struggles that we will go through when all the snow guns are making snow! (2) It will be extremely difficult to show emotions besides jumping down, clapping your hands, doing other body movements. Since every child seeks a beautiful smile of approval, you may want to temporarily lower the mask to show your smile. Science and technology are here to the rescue. Recently an innovative manufacturer has developed a unique-face mask that could assist all ski coaches with their lessons. It is a full-shield-clear plastic mask (To see your eyes and smiles) with an built-in amplifier to clearly hear your voice. (3) When you are skiing hard and seem to be out of breath, try lowering the mask and take two to three deep breaths to re oxygenate your lungs.

Other safety issues, for example, take the following into account:

---

[c] Ski Resorts Adjust, Hope Season Gets a Longer Run, "in USA Today, November 19, 2020, page 4D".

84

1. Do not coach your students under the chairlifts because of the possibility of falling equipment.

2. Coach them not to bomb the hill at mach-2 speed for fear of not being able to stop when a person unexpectedly changes direction in front of them. About 54 percent of the deaths occur on blue groomed runs; 31 percent are on were expert trails. Most of the accidents are males between the ages of eighteen and forty.

3. Emphasize slowing down into the lift line instead of zooming ahead so you do not have to spend extra time and energy skiing up to the next person in line or beating a person to the line.

4. Reduce the odds of getting into an accident by avoiding the section of the hill that is crowded or congested. Skiing and snowboarding are not contact sports; however, in reality, people do collide into one another. Minimize distractions; using ear buds to listen music or to take a mobile phone call can increase your risk for collisions.

5. Kids tend to play on the ride up on the chair. Avoid any unnecessary movements that can cause a student to slide off the chair; this is especially true when all the snow guns are making snow and the chair has snow on it and it freezes, making it extra slippery. It is always wise to pick up the tiny tots with your poles wrapped in front of them, lifting your student up with both hands holding each end of the poles tightly next to you. Even with teenagers, I still put my poles across their laps, hooked onto the armrest next to them to prevent any movement. This safety technique assures them that I care about them enough to ensure they don't get hurt. Children at this age are curious; make sure that the students do not try to see what is happening on the hill or chair behind them because they may twist out of the chair and fall; this important safety topic was discussed in greater detail in this chapter, under the topic, "Chairlift". It is becoming increasingly popular to carry a backpack, containing essentials such as water bottles, snacks, extra pair of goggles, cell phones, and radios. When riding the chairlifts, take the backpack off and place it in your lap. There have been reported cases of backpacks getting tangled on the back of the chairlift, resulting in accidents.

6. Avoid taking them into the terrain Park if you have not been trained to play in the park safely. About 27 percent of accidents occur in the terrain park, mostly due to freestyle exercises.

7. Ensure your students are cognitively, affectively, and physically ready to challenge themselves down a steeper terrain with the proper skills to go down in control and safely, especially on the last run when they are exhausted from the long lesson.

8. Never push your students beyond their mental and physical limits; this is especially true if they are tired or exhausted at the end of the lesson. Don't be afraid to stop for a short time-out even if the time of the lesson is not up.

9. Always check periodically that Maslow's Hierarchy of Needs, especially the physiological and safety needs, are being met; the child can be easily distracted and not obey what is being told when they have higher physiological or mental needs at the moment.

10. Pay special attention to those individuals that need more care, such as those with certain physical, mental, neurological disorders or diseases and those that are on special medications. Has your child been properly fed? Has he received his daily medications before going out on the slopes? Being a diabetic myself, I always keep a supply of rapidly-dissolving sugar cubes that dissolves rapidly in my pocket in case my sugar plummets. Some diabetic children keep sugar tabs or candy in their pockets in the event that hypoglycemia (Low-blood sugar) is eminent. Ideally, before taking any sugar product, I recommend testing the sugar level with a glucometer. Dropping blood sugar can result in the loss of cognition (Usually within a few minutes). Do try to understand the symptoms of low sugar in the blood (See chapter 7,, under "Diabetes"). Certainly, inform the parents of this incident. I also recommending a small pack of tissue in your pocket in the event a tiny tot needs any assistance with a runny nose. Winter time is flu season so, also keep a small bottle of hand sanitizer handy, especially in this era of new airborne viruses. Frequent disinfecting the hands *and* gloves will be the new norm. Little things like this can avoid distractions and can lead to a better outcome of a critical and challenging situation.

11. Teach the children how to carry their skis properly and safely when walking to and from the ski lodge. As this is a high-traffic area, be especially careful when changing direction so you do not hit someone else with the skis.

12. Never borrow someone else's skis; the DIN setting may not be correct for your height, weight, age, and skier performance level.

13. Another safety issue can be conquering fear[16] itself. Fear can be a terrifying thing, preventing a person from trying something new, causing them to sit back (The COM is behind the BOS), or letting emotions get out of hand and the child refuses any more instructions or wants to go back to their parents. Fear can, sometimes be good; promoting caution in dangerous circumstances, like a steeper slope or the terrain park. Some kids have no fear and can be a real hazard on the hill. As we get older, we file more fear factors and experiences into our brain. Some of the files are overfilled! You can keep the student on a lower terrain, doing different drills to hone in their skills. Eventually, that same terrain will become boring. Now, the challenge is to introduce the new steeper terrain. On the less-steep terrain, you may want to try fan turns. Tell the student to go straight down the fall line, bail out, and make a J- turn when fear begins to set in. As the straight runs get longer, the speed increases, but they can bail out and do a J-Turn. When the student understands that there is a safety net (By turning uphill), she can bail out of the calamity. Repeat that several more times to help concur their fears. Another exercise you can do on a less-steep terrain is to check their turn shapes (See figure 12).[5,16] Is it an S-shaped, C-shaped, or J-shaped curve? Some of the other fears are heights and speed. More on speed control is found in Chapter 8, Bag of Tricks.

Figure 12 Drawings of three different turn shapes[5, 16]"
S-shaped curve, C-shaped curve, J-shaped curve.

Going against gravity to slow down is key to controlling your speed, so understanding turn shapes is a mandate. The S-shaped curve should be reserved for more accomplished skiers, who can turn in control at a faster speed. The C-shaped curve should be taught to the beginner and intermediate skiers to help them move up the hill against gravity to slow down. Without slowing down, the body soon gets out of alignment with the skis, and compromises balance and the other skills. Turning then becomes a challenge.

One of the games which I like is to see which student can go down the slope the *slowest*, by making the most turns and completing the turns to slow down. I personally compete with them to add to the extra fun. The J-shaped turns are a good way to build confidence against fear. The fan-turn drill is excellent for this. As you well know, the fall-line is the fastest line for speed. The J-turn is an excellent way for the student to come to a complete stop. The super-large wedge should be reserved for emergency stops only, (i.e., In the lift line or in a crowded area when a hockey stop is not advised). Besides, a super-large wedge promotes the COM to remain in the back position causing imbalance. Figure 13 illustrates how staying in the fall line picks up speed, but one can bail out when the speed is excessive by making J-turns to come to a complete stop. This can be a good drill to help conquer fears of speed down the fall line.

I tell my students, "Speed causes injuries. That is why they have safe-speed limits in the city and on the highways. When your parents exceed the speed limits, they can get a speeding ticket and you can get one too from the ski patrol. So, always ski safely by going slow."

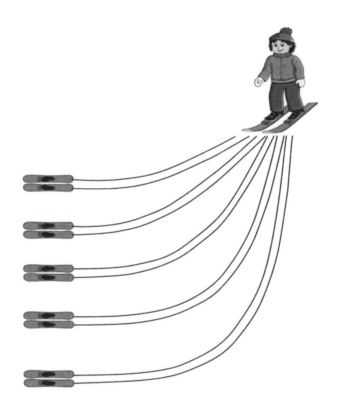

Figure 13: Fan turns; making different size J-turns to help conquer fear of speed[5]

Have you ever experienced students getting bored in your intermediate class? Did you then decide to take them into the terrain park? Why not? You can teach them to do the wave, do small jumps, and do the tables. Teach them to do 360-degree turns on the ground. They will love the fun associated with the park. The key to success in the Terrain Park[34, 43] is to carefully explain the safety rules when in the park.[34, 43] Always make each and every one of them examines the park before actually doing their stunts.

The terrain park is a marvelous place to take the kids to have fun. However, it is a dangerous area to ski in because of the many potential hazards. I cannot overemphasize the importance of safety for the kids, especially the first-timers. Be Smart, think smart, and coach smart. In fact, use the PSIA Smart Style guide.[33, 34]

S = Start Small; do simple maneuvers first

M = Make a Plan; carefully scope the park and decide

A = Always look before you leap

R = Respect gets respect

T = Take it easy; easy style it

Tell the children where the potential hazards are and what they should do to minimize any possible accidents. Also, wave out or signal each student down one by one as they go over the bumps and jumps, making sure that everyone has completed their turn safely. Then select one person (In rotation) to be at a critical and potential hazardous juncture to observe each student compete their turn safely.

Inform your kids about the no-zones or no-stopping areas. As a coach, you should know what hand or pole signals or symbols (i.e., "O" for open, "X" for closed) that you can use to communicate with Snow Sport enthusiasts at the top of the hill. Coaches should know the ATML Model[34, 43] before taking their students into the park.

A = Approach phase entails everything the person does before transitioning into the takeoff phase, including knowing what maneuver they are going to do and making the necessary preparation (e.g., Speed, direction, timing) before they approach the take-off ramp.

T = Takeoff phase refers to the movements at or near the lip of the feature. This is the most intense part of the journey, and the student should have a solid knowledge of the fundamentals.

M = Maneuver phase includes a child's movements and stance in the air between takeoff and landing (e.g., Checking the amount of air on a table or pipe wall, sliding on a rail or even while performing simple jibs on the flats).

L = Landing phase refer to the movements that are necessary to complete a safe drop from the air.

Be sure you start on low-pitched groomers, banks or sidewalls, cat tracks, wind lips, natural rolls. Demonstrate the switch, ollies, jibs, presses, butters, bonks, and spins.

Some tips for teaching freestyle in the terrain park:

- Make an inspection run through the park.
- Clear features for students before they ride.
- Start small and work up to more difficult and dynamic stunts.
- Always apply proper class management and safety.

Photo 26. A seven-year-old boy doing small jump in the terrain park with good fundamentals of skiing.[46]

If you see a high embankment in the terrain park (On a cat track), use it to your advantage. I particularly like to take kids having difficulty breaking away from a wedge to use the embankment. To have fun, I will tell them, "Let's have a contest; those that get to the top or the highest height will be my patrol leader!" I will tell

91

the child that is still in a wedge, "Hey, let me tell you a secret. If you do French fries instead of a pizza, you will get up higher." They not only have fun with this activity, but it will help them break away from the wedge and move on to parallel skiing.

In case of an **Accident**, the following **Rules** should be observed:

- Do not touch or move the injured person.
- Do not remove any of their equipment.
- Ask someone to tell the lift operator to call the ski patrol.
- Stay with the student.

Put your skis in an "X" high above the injured person to prevent a collision from oncoming traffic.

Have the hill supervisor (Or other management staff member) appoints another instructor to take over the class.

Accompany the injured student to the skip patrol hut to complete the necessary paper work.

Try to immediately locate the child's parents to inform them of the accident; call the front desk at the resort (Follow the resort policy).

Do not overlook your kids' preparation for the snow. Many parents do not know the fundamentals of preparing their child for their first snow sport lesson. As their coach you need to inform both the parent and child of the essentials of dressing for blizzard conditions, sub-zero weather, the elements of the wind, blowing snow from the snow guns, rain, and so on. Here is a brief checklist when preparing for the outdoors (More detailed information is provided in Chapter 4, under "safety"):

The concept of layering the clothing: base layer, mid-layer, outer layer that is windproof, waterproof. and can breathable (See discussion on clothing in this chapter).

Pay attention to the material composition selected: wool, silk, and synthetic materials help with the wicking process and to help retain body heat. Do not use cotton materials.

Socks should preferably be changed just before the lesson. The feet are continuously perspiring, some kids' feet more than others. If you put the ski socks on before they leave the house, many times they will be damp with perspiration, which will lead to cold feet when on the snow on a bitter cold day.

Warm weather during the spring lessons, may require removing the outer layer; be prepared with the proper mid-layer to keep them warm but not hot. I say you should consider the outer layer first because many times, it is made up of down feathers, which can be great for bitter cold weather but not for warm spring-weather skiing. Alternatively, if they are wearing a thinner outer shell, you can remove one of the mid-layers.

Make sure that the pants and gloves are waterproof and windproof because they are most likely to get wet. Be sure that the pants and gloves are breathable to minimize the accumulation of perspiration.

Be sure they their neck area are protected from the elements; avoid scarves and wraps for safety reasons because they can get tangled on the chairlift and prevent the person from unloading. A turtle-neck sweater can do the job. Because of the COVID-19 pandemic, you may want to consider recommending to the child to wear a full-cover balaklava, which will protect the entire face and neck area. The goggles will protect the eyes and the rest of the face.

Neoprene face masks are always helpful for subzero weather. They are usually thicker than the balaclava fabric and will help protect most of the face, head, and ears from the cold, and even from frostbite.

Inform them of the many uses of a properly fitted helmet. It doesn't take much to obtain a concussion; snow sport is an active sport. I ask the parent, "How much do value your child's brain? Is it worth more than a one-hundred-dollar helmet?" A child will lose 60 percent of their body heat via the head. The helmet will help keep your child warmer. It is always wise to purchase helmets with adjustable vents to allow heat to escape when the weather gets warmer.

Check their goggles. Are they the correct size and shape to fit the contour of their faces. Goggles not only keep a large portion of their face warmer, but also keeps the flying snow and other particles from getting into their eyes.

Know the signs of frostbite (See chapter 4, "Frostbite"). This is a very common and serious problem. I would like to spend more time on this important subject because

1. Children are particularly susceptible because of several reasons:
   Children lose heat from their skin (Particularly from their head) much faster than adults because of their head-to-body ratio is larger in kids as compared to adults.
2. Kids can get so excited and engrossed in playing in the snow that they lose track of what is happening to their bodies, or simply ignore how cold or uncomfortable they continue to have uninterrupted fun.
3. A child may not have the cognitive skills at three- or four-year old (Or even eight-years-old) as compared to a kid over the age of thirteen, to alert them to the symptoms of frostbite and how to prevent them (i.e., Taking a break and seeking warm shelter).

Because of these reasons, parents should especially be attentive to the following: (1) monitoring the weather forecast, outdoor temperature, wind velocity, wind-chill factor, (2) asking frequent questions from the knowledgeable coach, (3) allowing and expecting periodic warm up time in a warm shelter and offer warm fluids and food.

Frostnip and frostbite can be a common occurrence in this Winter sport. Frostbite refers to freezing of the body skin and underlying tissues caused by extreme cold. This can result in the loss of feeling and color in the tissues. There are three degrees of frostbite:

- Frostnip: white patches of skin that are numb.

- Superficial frostbite: skin that is white and hard; deeper skin, blood vessels, and nerve injury with a burning and stinging sensation; clear water-filled blisters that may develop when the skin is rewarmed.

- Deep frostbite: grayish-yellow or blue skin and feels hard or waxy; larger blood vessels and nerves, muscles, tendons, and bone injury occur with the loss of sensation; gangrene and infection may develop.

What should you do? First of all, *prevention* is key. Recognize the symptoms and take quick action. Check the exposed areas of the skin; is there redness, or any other color or lack of color? Skin with frostnip starts out being red and later turns pale, cold and hard with no feeling. Does the child feel "pins and needles"? This sensation is followed by numbness and this may lead to an early throbbing or aching feeling but later, on the affected parts, feels like a block of wood. Do they show signs of being cold? It's time to bring them in immediately! The most common areas of the body affected include the fingers and toes (Which account for 90 percent of the cases). Nose, lips, cheeks and ears follow. Some medical conditions such as diabetes, peripheral vascular disease, Renaud's syndrome, hypothyroidism (Low thyroid function), some forms of heart problems can result in increased susceptibility to frostbites. Be especially attentive when the snow guns are blowing sticky snow, which adheres to the body. The high winds and cold can potentially add to increased risk of Frostnip or Frostbite.

To summarize the symptoms of frostbite:

- Redness of the skin
- Loss of skin color
- Blue skin color
- Graying or blackening of the affected areas
- Feeling 'pins and needles'
- Local numbness
- Local blisters
- Local swelling
- Shivering
- Slurred speech
- Memory loss

Be aware, a child with frostbite on the extremities may also be subjected to hypothermia (Lowered body-core temperature). Check for hypothermia and treat these symptoms first. In this instance, call the ski patrol or admit the kid to the emergency room. Also, if your child has had frostnip or frostbite previously, the child will be five-times more sensitive to the cold and more prone to have a repeated event.

What should you do for Treatment? Work swiftly:

- Get the child out of the wind and cold.
- Move the child to a warm shelter.
- Remove any wet or damp clothing, mittens, or socks when you get indoors.
- Remove any constricting jewelry.
- Remove any tight clothing or clothing that may restrict blood flow.
- Apply slow warming with blankets and warm clothing.
- Do NOT rub or massage the frostbitten areas.
- Do NOT let the child walk on the frostbitten feet.
- Do NOT apply any direct heat to the area.
- Do NOT sit by a warm fire.
- Do NOT warm the child with an electric blanket.
- Do NOT break the blisters.
- Do provide ample warm fluids.
- Preventive antibiotic medications may be necessary per the advice of the doctor.
- Pain medications may be necessary.
- Treatment for general hypothermia may be necessary.

Common sense should dictate when and where the extreme cold weather forecast is in the making. As their coach, you need to take the leadership in preventing these types of mishaps.

Allergies:

This is a growing problem and concern. According to the Centers for Disease Control and Prevention[d], 34 percent of the respondents in a survey reacted to food allergens in a restaurant. I bring this topic up because much of the food consumption at the food court at the ski resorts are catered or homemade, and the customer cannot see the labels.

---

d From www.foodallergy.org on May 30, 2019.

Allergy is a condition in which a person's immune system overreacts to substances known as allergens and releases chemicals called histamines, which causes the symptoms. **Common allergens** are:

- *Foods.* Nuts (Peanuts, cashews, walnuts), shellfish (Shrimp, lobster, crab), fish, sesame seeds (Commonly found in bagels and Asian foods), certain legumes (Lentils, peas, soy beans), dairy (Milk, yogurt, eggs).
- *Insects.* Many flying insects (Stings from honeybees, yellow jackets, wasps, hornets), ticks can cause severe allergic reaction, called anaphylaxis shock.
- *Medications.* Penicillin and many antibiotics, chemotherapy, muscle relaxants, pain relievers (Aspirin, ibuprofen, nonsteroidal anti-inflammatory drugs), latex-related products (Balloons, gloves) are common allergens.
- *Contact dermatitis.* Clothing (Certain natural fabrics and dyes) are common.
- *Pollens.* Many trees, weeds, plants and grasses release pollens that will cause hay fever.
- *Mold and dust mites.* These are the biggest allergy triggers in the Fall.
- *Animals.* The fur or hair, saliva, urine, and dander (Dried flakes of skin).

Many of the allergies are benign, and others are life-threatening. Let's look the symptoms presented by these two categories:

A. Benign symptoms:
- Nasal Congestion
- Itchy and Watery eyes
- Sneezing
- Stuffy or runny nose
- Scratchy or sore throat
- Cough from post-nasal drip
- Phlegm
- Drowsiness

B. Some life-threatening allergies— Anaphylaxis warning signs:
- Breathing difficulties
- Low blood pressure
- Change in consciousness
- Chest pain or tightness, and trouble swallowing.

- Hives, swelling of the lips and other areas of the body, a tingling feeling, itchiness, or skin rash.
- Nausea, vomiting, dizziness, diarrhea, and stomach cramps.

One needs to respond swiftly if you recognize some of these life-threatening symptoms. Do you know how to use the Epinephrine pen? Be sure that you know where the child is carrying the **Epinephrine pen** and know to use it in an emergency.

Helmet:

Another area of safety often times neglected is the informed choice of helmet selection. Common cause of injury in snow sport include falling down, being hit by someone else, or hitting an object or another person on the hill. Unfortunately, a person colliding into your child happens about 6.4 percent of the reported accidents to the ski patrol. Who knows the number of unreported cases?

Helmets can help protect the child's brain in low-impact collisions and falls. Helmet use has been documented to reduce the incidence of any head injury 30 to 50 percent, but the decrease in head injuries is generally limited to the less serious injuries, such as scalp lacerations, mild concussions (Grade I), and contusions to the head, as opposed to more serious injuries like a concussion greater than Grade II, skull fractures, open head injuries, and the like. Once you get a concussion, you are five times more likely to run the risk of another subsequent concussion! The age groups most susceptible to injury are those under twenty-six or over fifty years, beginners, intermediates, and snowboarders. People involved in a collision were more likely to injure their head than those who just fall by themselves. Terrain parks were the areas on the slopes that were prime territories for head injuries.

The most recent helmet usage data clearly indicate that skiers and snowboarders already understand the importance of using helmets on the slope. According to the 2019-2020 National Ski Areas Association data, 57 percent of the snow sports enthusiasts use helmets. The data also show that 87 percent of children nine years or younger are wearing helmets; 75 percent of children between ten and fourteen- years wear helmets, and 70 percent of adults over the age of sixty-five years wear head protection. Because of the many recent news stories on concussions suffered on the football field, we suspect that the percentage of users have markedly increased. Ski resorts will eventually make it mandatory, and a skier or snowboarder will not be able to enter the slopes. Helmets have a limited life span. Please inform the parents that they should not use hand-me-down helmets from the older child to the younger one or receive an old helmet from another family member. The fit may be wrong, or the helmet is outdated.

Helmets come in various styles and shapes. Among these are full shell, three-quarter shell, and full-face models. Full shell models provide more coverage (Including the ears) and protection, but they can get hot on warmer days. While cost is a major factor, make sure that the helmet is approved by CEN 1077, SSTM, or Snell organizations to ensure high-performance standards and impact specifications. Snell has the highest standards of approval, while CEN has the lowest approved standards. Comfort and fit are both important when selecting a helmet; color may also be a factor. The fit should be snug but not tight. I too often observe a child wearing an inappropriately fitted helmet that sits close to the front hairline; a properly fitted helmet should cover the frontal lobe (Halfway down the forehead). The child has probably outgrown the helmet.

According to research data, a helmet loses its full protection after the first couple of impacts- time to throw it away. Research and development are continuously discovering new materials that can better absorb impact, and new designs that can be more protective. For instance, some manufactures use back protectors or bumpers that are molded to the body of the helmet and also provide more comfort. Other manufacturers design helmets with multi-directional strike-protection system, which is designed to redirect and reduce the impact even from an indirect hit. The helmet involves a low-friction layer inside the helmet over which the outer helmet moves after the impact. As helmets evolve, the manufactures will offer helmets that can reduce concussions. Do not be under the illusion that your child is safe just because the child is wearing a helmet. There are other careless individuals on the hill that are reckless; even worse, they do not know the safety rules and may collide into your kid. You may want to consider a helmet color that is unique and bright (e.g., Orange or lime green, instead of the standard black, grey, or white). Most helmets cost around $65 to $350, depending on the amenities (e.g., Design of the helmets, having ventilation vents, having more padding, more functional ear flaps for better sound conduction and even with Bluetooth technology).

Ski Goggles:

Not all ski goggles have the same contour to match the contour of the specific brand and model of the helmet. While you're in the ski shop purchasing a helmet, you may want to consider buying ski goggles that match the front contour of the helmet. There should be no gaps between the goggles and helmet. The strap of the goggles must be able to go outside the helmet, where it can be attached to a device at the back of the helmet to prevent run-away gear. The goggles will not only help protect the eyes from the cold, wind, sun, and snow but give added protection from injury and the COVID-19 virus.

Lens choices are many. The color of the lens can affect the percentage of visual transmitted light that reaches your eyes. A clear or light pink- or rose-colored lens should be used at night and a dark or mirrored lens such as platinum, gray, black and red are suitable during bright light during the day. They usually have a VTL or 25% or less. Overcast or cloudy skies require yellow, gold/copper, amber, or rose-colored lenses; the VTL is 50% or greater. Then, there are specialized lenses with enhanced lens technology to help you see details on the snow to respond quicker to the terrain conditions. Specific dyes are used in the lenses which manipulate the light spectrum to filter out noisy colors, while simultaneously enhancing the color that your eyes are responsive. The lens technology has advanced to the point where some high-tech lenses will automatically change from low VTL to high VTL. One final comment about goggles safety concerns effectiveness of fog removal. Some goggles are designed to remove the trapped fog between the face and goggle better than others. Most goggles have a thin anti-fog coating on the inside of the lens. Do not rub the inside of the lens when it gets wet with an abrasive cloth. This will not only scratch the lens, but also remove the thin anti-fog coating.

Ski Boots:

What about the most important ski gear, boots? Safety can be an issue if they are improperly fitted. All too often, a parent will get hand-me-downs or purchase boots at a swap meet or second-hand store. Most of the time they are too big! Ski rentals can make the same mistake. The kid is swimming in those monstrous clunkers, resulting in their inability to properly move their feet in the boots or remain balance during their movements, which will compromise their safety. The boots should fit snuggly but not tightly. Many times, kids will complain with the slightest pressure on the feet when you tighten the boots down with the buckles. Have the kid present the child's hands to you and shake it with a *firm* grip. That's the relative snugness he/she should tolerate and feel. As the feet move (i.e., Tilt on to outside edge of the foot or inside edge of the foot, the skis should immediately respond, not with a delayed action.

When the weather gets bitter cold, I have observed some unaware students wearing double socks to keep warm. This should never be done because the foot with the feet with the first sock will *slide* in the second sock causing one to be out of balance. Instead purchase a good quality ski sock made of Merino wool.

Fitting a boot properly is an art and a science. It takes many years of experience to learn the trade. Start by measuring the foot with a foot-measuring tool, usually marked in Mondo size, which is universally used throughout the world. The shell comes in full sizes and the liner in half-sizes.

Table 1
Boot Sizes

USA Kids Size	Mondo Size
7	13.5
8	14.5
9	15.5
10	16.5
11	17.5
12	18.5
13	19.5
1	20.5
2	21.5
3	22
4.5	22.5
5	23
5.5	23.5
6	24.5
7	25
8	26.5

The boots have a hard plastic (Different kinds and types to adjust for the softness or hardness) outer shell and a soft inner liner, which can pack out in a matter of one hundred ski days. When selecting kids' boots you have two options: (1) Top entry boot, which is the traditional boot. It may take come effort to getting the little feet inside. (2) Rear entry boot, which tends to be a bit easier to get on, especially for the tiny tots. Start with a shell fit; check to see the amount of room available on each side of the feet and behind the heel. With the liner out of the shell, place the kid's foot (With proper ski socks on) into the shell and check the spacing between the shell and outside edge of the foot and the inside edge of the foot (A one-finger width) and the amount of spacing behind the heel of the boot (About a two-finger width). The liner will take up a one-finger width when it is placed back into the shell. The extra-finger width behind the heel will allow for future growth. Without buckling anything, teach the child the proper way and sequence to put the boots on. It is important that the child understands how to get the child's heel all the way back into the back pocket of the boot, by forcibly tapping the heel down onto the ground at an angle that will allow the heel to slide back. Then use the buckle closest to the ankle and tighten down to keep the heel in the heel pocket. Next, tighten the rest of the foot buckles and then the power strap, if there is one. The fit is appropriate if the front toes are just touching the front of the boot while the child is standing and the toes should pull back away from the front of the boot when the child flexes (Pressing on the tongue of the boot to push the knees forward) to create an athletic stand. There should be no other materials (Ski pants, long johns, etc.) in the boot other than the ski socks (To prevent any pinching due to overlapping of the materials) or any hot spots when the boot buckles are clamped down. A return visit may be required to adjust for the hotspots or newly created blisters. The liner has a life of forty to one hundred ski days or two to five years if the kid skis 20 days a year. When the liner becomes overly compacted, the foot will feel loose in the boot. Many times, a loosely fitted boot will cause blisters because of excessive foot movements in the boot. It's time to buy a new boot.

Photo 27. A three-year-old girl in a pair of boots that
is a tad too big. (You think?)

SKIS

The evolution of ski design has resulted in more shaped and shorter skis for quicker mobility, quicker turning, and more stability through the turns. Over the years, the performance characteristics of skis of different brands have differed little. When I worked for the largest retail store in the Midwest, I was selected to go out to an Upper Michigan ski resort with the store's research team to purchase the store's following year's inventory. We spent three full days evaluating each ski's (1) graphics, (2) turn initiation ease, (3) stability at low and high speeds, (4) performance in crud, in powder, and on ice, (5) performance as a short-radius, medium-radius, and large-radius turning skis, (6) performance as a free-style, mogul, and race ski, and (7) other unique features, including lightness, tip-swing weight, quickness, and construction. Be mindful that each brand and model have their own unique fingerprint that makes skis outstanding.

In general, especially children's skis, pay attention to the softness of the skis, ski lenght (Beginner skiers should have shorter than typical skis for easier maneuverability), ski weight, ski shape (The more hourglass shaped the easier to turn). Be mindful, some parents may purchase skis that are older and are more straight shaped. These older skis may require the skills or an instructor who knows how to maximize straight-skis performance[48]. Also, be aware that skis that are older than ten years cannot have their bindings-release check done at the ski shop because the manufacturers will not allow it. Be aware, as a ski instructor, you are not allowed to adjust the ski bindings because you may not be certified.

Ski Poles:

For the Beginner, the ski poles are *not* recommended because of the possible distractions to the tiny tikes during skiing, and while getting onto and off the people-mover carpet or chairlifts. It is only when they reach towards the end of the intermediate performance zone that the coach should recommend to parents that they get ski poles for their child. Selecting ski poles is an ever-changing process as the child grows. You might suggest to the parents that they to consider purchasing adjustable poles; they are a bit more expensive, but in the long run, they will be ahead. The proper size of the ski poles should be determined by holding the ski poles upside down, then gripping just under the ski basket. It is a proper fit if the forearm is parallel to the ground. Place an address label (With a name and telephone number) somewhere on the poles in case they are forgotten at the ski school. Poles can be dangerous; never have the child pointing the baskets of the poles with the tips directly in front of her because they can poke someone ahead of her or even injure her if the butt of the poles jabs her. Be sure to teach how to use the ski-pole straps properly to prevent injuries; 5 percent of ski injuries are the result of ski-pole accidents. I'll discuss the proper use of ski poles in chapter 9.

Proper Clothing

For clothing, educate the parents and students that "an ounce of prevention is worth a pound of cure." Protection from the elements is essential. Dressing with several thin layers is better than one bulky piece of clothing. Layering properly is noteworthy:

Layer one or the base layer. This is the layer that sits next to your skin. It needs to wick moisture (Absorb and move the moisture outward and away from the body), not trap it. Cotton fabric will trap the moisture, so, it is not the appropriate fabric to use. Synthetics like polyester blends (i.e., Polypropylene) are good choices. Natural materials such as wool and silk are also excellent choices. Socks should never be cotton; ski and snowboard socks have special materials that help wick perspiration from the feet away from the body.

Layer two or the middle layer. This layer is the workhouse. Traditionally, this layer is bulky because it has the job of holding in warm air (Which is the best insulator) and moving the wicked moisture away from the first layer. The best materials for the mid-layer for the money are synthetics. A non-pulling fleece

Layer three or the outer layer. This layer is the shell (Jacket or pants), which should keep out the rain, wind, and snow. Many manufactures print IP ratings on the marketing tags (e.g., 5,000 mm to 20,000 mm). The higher the rating, the higher the waterproofing and breathability of the garment. There are also special tricks when buying ski pants. You might want to suggest to parents that there are some brands of ski pants that have adjustable hems that can be adjusted to the proper length as their kids grow. Don't forget turtleneck sweaters; they are highly recommended to protect their necks, especially in frigid weather. Don't forget the face mask and/or balaclava to help protect the face from the cold and air-borne viruses.

How many times have you observed your student wearing inexpensive gloves that are not waterproof? A good glove should be warm enough to cover the cold temperatures in your area, breathable so that it doesn't trap moisture, and waterproof because they will fall and get their gloves wet in the snow. When preparing your child for their ski lesson, inform the parents that they need to always check the upcoming weather forecast. What was the forecast for the amount of snow that was dumped on the ground, and how much more do you expect? What will be the temperature going to be when your child has an advanced-booked lesson? What will the wind-chill factor be? Will there be a blizzard-like conditions? Will it be raining? Will there be sunshine? In some areas of the country where ski resorts are at higher elevations and have more sunshine, be sure that the parents have applied sunscreen to their child's face because of the high UV Index.

Photo 28. Three properly dressed boys playing outside with their ski instructor making snowballs to have some fun.

 Knowing how to protect your students under all circumstances is your primary goal as a ski coach. Be sure to check their understanding of safety; when and how to by various techniques.

CHAPTER 5

Developing a Strong Foundation—Using Proper Tools and Props

The number of tools and props that you can use to assist your coaching is endless.[2-5, 9, 12-15,16,33,34,46,47] They can only inhibit you from using them in your coaching because of availability, your money to purchase them, and your ingenuity. Whenever possible, use these gadgets to enhance your kids' skiing experiences and to help accelerate the learning curve. They can also be useful to ensure safety and fun during the lessons. The key is knowing your product (i.e., How to use them, what their limitations are, and when and where to use them).

It can be helpful for your kids if you set up a children's theme park filled with large cutouts, handmade-carpet-covered wooden ramps for side-stepping, arches so that they can flex and extend while attempting to go under the bridge, and obstacle courses so that they can practice rotating their legs to avoid objects that are in their way. Large air-filled animals can also be used so that they can have fun moving with their skis throughout the park. I like using simple and inexpensive tools, such as a small horn that you can carry in your pocket can be fun. I can use it to let kids know they did something correctly. Letting everyone know you are coming by honking all the way down the hill can be a rewarding and unique experience for kids. I also like carrying small hand puppets or finger puppets to entertain them on the chairlifts. For these kids, *creativity* is the name of the game; so use as many different toys, tools and games as you can during your lesson.

Let me share with you an example of fun and creativity. Anabel was a four-year old girl who came for her first ski lesson. She was extremely shy and as quiet as a mouse. I told Anabel, "I am Pineapple Herb. I just want to clown around to have tons of fun on the snow."

I put on my red and green clown wig. She started to laugh at me. I started honking my horn and started dancing around, taking her hand to dance with me. To my glee, she took my hand and walked out of the lodge on to the snow. I also asked her if she would like Coco the Flying Monkey to ride on her back as we skied.

She said, "oh boy, yes!"

Was she ever so excited! The purpose of using Coco was to entertain her and, more importantly, to have her bend from the hips to achieve a slight angle on her back (About thirty degrees) to achieve an athletic stance for better balance on the skis. I told her, "If you stand upright, Coco will slide down her back, but if she tilts her back a little, the Flying Monkey will be able to hang on for the ride."

We worked on her athletic stance by having her "knees ahead of the toes and nose ahead of the toes," by having her back slanted from the hips about thirty degrees (So that when it rains, it rolls off her back). I also told her, I'm going to place a one hundred-dollar bill in each of your boots between her shin and the tongue of the boot. If she keeps pressing on the one-hundred bill", (I used green paper money), "It will never fly out and get lost, and you won't have to pay me back" (See figure 18), when a person has their calf touching the back of the boot). I explained to the dad where we would meet after the lesson and where he could watch our lesson unfold. Anabel and I pretended to skate on ice, making figure eights and big, fat circles. I set up two ski poles about ten feet apart, and we raced from one pole to the next. Then, we made a pizza and did a gliding wedge, all the while fine-tuning her balance by examining where her COM was relative to her BOS. Her cognitive, affective, and physical developments were all 9. Later, I told Anabel, "Let's make some French Fries instead of pizza and slowly go down the hill" (Four-foot runoffs)." Next, we worked on side steps, climbing up the hill (About ten feet). We made small J-turns and a mixture of different turn shapes. I took out a small hand puppet (Grumpy Bear) to whisper in my ear.

She said, "What did the bear say?"

I said, "I can't tell you because it is a secret that we have as buddies."

Anabel said, "Please, tell me, please. I'll be your friend too, and I won't tell anyone, even my best friend, Laura."

I said, "Okay, Grumpy Bear said he wanted you to go slightly faster and weave in and out of the flags placed on the hill."

After learning to link wedge turns, we went down the slope with six small flags in the snow. I gave her a lot of high fives. I asked Anabel, "What did you think about your first ski lesson?"

She said, "I liked it, NO...I loved it! I'm going to tell Dad that I want you again for my next lesson."

Her homework was on edging-, pressure-,rotational-control and balance by walking sideways like a crab for ten minutes every day, up a hill and down a hill. Her reward was a gift from the dollar store (That week, it was a small teddy bear). I was booked with Anabel for the rest of the ski season. The point of this story is, an instructor must be creative and must be able to find ways to excite them. *Fun* should be a high priority in your lessons; having the kids do fun games without them knowing that they are actually learning proper skiing movements with their bodies so that the skis to respond appropriately should be the goal of every ski instructor. With all the resources that are available, try to learn the craft to be creative and innovative with the props and games.

As a member of the Ed Staff, I always marvel at the kid's coaches that we train, who take to take to heart what they learned in the many workshops and clinics. They're the ones that excel as coaches and implement the skills and fundamentals of skiing into their lesson plans with much creativity and fun. The outcome is that these teachers obtain more accolades from their customers and parents, have more rewards, and have more requested private lessons.

These are some of the common props an instructor can be use:

- ski-tip connectors to make a wedge
- plastic Hoops
- ski Harnesses
- poles
- puppets and stuffed animals
- cones
- strips of carpet or rugs

- flying Disc
- bridges
- horn

I will give a brief description of each to demonstrate why, how, when, and where we can properly use them to our advantage. Several photographs will be presented in this section to illustrate the usefulness of the props.

Ski-tip connector. Before a discussion is presented on these wonderful wedge-holding devices. I would like to ask the question: Why teach the wedge for beginning students the wedge? Why not just teach direct-to-parallel skiing? There are three reasons why: (1) the wedge is a more stable platform for balance then parallel skiing, (2) It is a method of slowing the students down, (3) the mechanics we teach for the wedge turns can be applied to parallel turns. The ski-tip connecting tool can be used for the toddlers (Ages three to six years old), who cannot make or hold a wedge, and it minimizes the chances of the tips of the skis crossing over each, which can cause locking of the skis. Any of these factors can compromise balance, which will affect their skiing. Using the CAP model, tiny tots may not have the physical and cognitive skills to make a wedge. Neurologically and muscularly, the little ones may not have the muscle coordination and strength to make a wedge, let alone different size wedges (See photo 29). Thus, this tool may help toddlers with overcoming some of their challenges (e.g., Fear of speed).

Photo 29. Three-year-old girl using a ski-tip connector to assist her
in making and maintaining a wedge platform going down the hill.

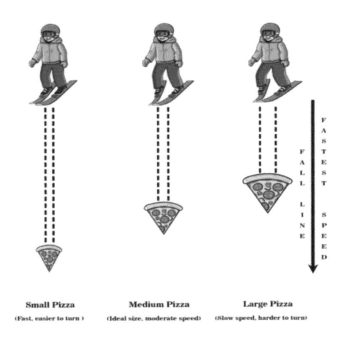

Small Pizza
(Fast, easier to turn)

Medium Pizza
(Ideal size, moderate speed)

Large Pizza
(Slow speed, harder to turn)

Figure 14. Drawing: pictures of three different size Pizzas that the child can use to regulate the relative speed

What is an ideal size wedge? An ideal wedge size for all children and adults is a wedge in which the BOS is hip width in the center of the skis. There are several kinds of wedges-enhancing devices that can be purchased for a little money. There are those with a thumbscrew to tighten the ski-tip connector onto the tips of the ski. There are those with a clamp. I prefer the latter because it is easier to use, and it is more convenient to use (Especially in severely cold weather) and also when you need to quickly remove them (i.e., When they have to move from point A to point B, like climbing up the hill or when they use the people-mover conveyer belt or when they need to use the chairlift). They come in different sizes and length. Every coach should have at least one ski-tip connector in their pocket.

Plastic Hoops

This tool comes in different sizes and tubular strength and are inexpensive. You can use them for various tasks. If a three- or four-year old struggles to stay upright on the skis, focus on balance. Pull him/her (With the plastic hoop placed behind his/her lower back, and pulling him/her on a flat terrain, with some bumps included. This same technique can be used to pull the child up the slope. Some kids cannot do side steps to climb the hill, or if they do, they will be exhausted after a while, and it takes enormous time out of your allotted teaching time. When you can use this to pull the child, grab the plastic hoop, and pull him/her, but be sure you check her body alignment and check if her COS is centered over his/her BOS. He/She should be in an athletic stance, with his/her hands out in front of him/her. You can even use them on the beginner slopes to control his/her speed and assist her turns as you go down the slope.

Photo 30. A plastic hoop is being used to control the child's speed and to assist him to stand in balance and guide him as he makes a few turns.

Photo 31. A four-year-old boy is being pulled up the hill with a plastic hoop.

Ski Harnesses

Ski harnesses are a great must-have tool. They are a lifesaver in conquering children's fears and for controlling their speed. There are several varieties available. There are those that have a vest with a hand-lift strap high on the back and the holding straps (Reins, usually eight to ten feet long). I do not like the ones which the lifting handle attached high up on the torso with the reins coming off that handle because this tends to hold the kid's upper body (COM) back behind the BOS, causing the child to be out of balance. However, they are particularly useful for lifting a tiny tot up on the chairlift. I suggest using those with a strap around the lower waist close to the hips with the reins (Straps) directly behind. I particularly like using this tool whenever I have doubts about a child being able to make a turn, complete a turn, or initiate a new turn without picking up too much speed. I even use harnesses on young adults. So, you may want several different sizes that are adjustable around the lower waist. I usually keep the one with the smaller waist adjustment in my jacket pocket at all times. When using the harnesses, I tell the child, "You are the unicorn horse. I'll tug the rein on the left side several times to give you the signal to turn left, and vice versa. When I tug the rein on the right, it is the signal to turn right." It is important not to keep the reins tight at all times; give them enough slack to give them the freedom to ski by themselves. Only when the speed is too excessive should you tighten up the reins to get them to regroup and get their body alignment correct to be in better balance. Many times, after several runs from top to bottom on the beginner hill with the harness, I will let go of the harness on the lower part of the slope to observe how well the child is doing the controlled wedge-turns turns down the hill. This allows me to give the child accurate feedback immediately after the run. For example, I focus on whether or not the child is using the proper body movements to get the skis to turn in link turns as he/she skis in control, down the slope. Use as much of the hill as possible. Be sure to check the child's speed using transition turns by going across the hill, side to side, rather than going straight down the hill in a narrow path. Harnesses are also useful when teaching kids to make parallel turns because the first part of the turn (Parallel skis before the fall line) can be daunting. This way, you can control the child's speed and fears when they execute the parallel turns. I have hand-made harness large enough to use even with adults for this purpose.

Photo 32. A ski harness is being used on a four-year –old girl to slow her down as she weaves through the cones, which is simulating a race course.

All too often, I see coaches not using harnesses and instead substitute the harness by holding the student from the rear (By holding onto their jacket). Unfortunately, this technique tends to cause the child to lean back onto that support system and causes that child to be out of balance.

Photo 33. A five-year-old boy is leaning back onto the coach's hands for support, which causes the boy's COM to fall behind his BOS.[46]

Poles

Bamboo, hard plastic, and ski poles are extremely useful tools to use in a ski lesson to help with controlling a student's speed and for assisting with their turns. I will discuss four different approaches to the proper use of the poles. I will also include the pros and cons of each technique.

Bamboo and hard plastic poles are used a lot by instructors because it is widely available (Orange stakes used to keep posted signs and emergency nets are setup). These poles are usually between six to eight feet long. These longer poles have the advantage of providing a better view of what the skis are doing and how the student's body movements are affecting the skis. On the downside, the instructor needs to get the pole from the storage area and bring it out to the training area and return it to the storage area after the lesson. Another disadvantage is that the long pole is cumbersome when loading and unloading the chairlift with multiple toddlers.

Many instructors improvise by using their ski poles because they are readily available and convenient. There are several ways that they can be used. A common way is to keep the poles on the child's lower waist and have them execute the turns while the instructor is directly behind the student. In another technique, like the bamboo and hard plastic poles method, the child is skiing alongside of the coach by holding on to his two poles, but the view of the skis and student's body movements are somewhat restricted compared to the long-pole method (See photo 34). Another technique is for the coach to ski backward and have the poles extended in a horizontal position in front so the child can grab on to it and maneuver down the hills (See photo 35). The advantage of the technique is you are eye to eye with your student for more effective communication. However, this method requires "eyes behind the coach's head" to avoid colliding with another person. I have seen this too often. In addition, this style of pole use has the added disadvantage of not being able to see what the child's skis and lower body movements are doing. A minor variation of this technique is having the child hold on to the handle end of the poles while and the ski instructor extends the child's arms straight out; this method has a slight advantage over the previous method because the coach can get a better view on how the skis and child's body are maneuvering (See photo 36). Like the previous method, you have direct eye-to-eye contact, but with only a slightly better view of the skis and lower-body movements. With this method, I have witnessed a slight issue when trying to complete the C-turn. For example, if you have an eighteen-year-old kid that weighs 185 pounds with a 115 pounds instructor, the coach will have less stability maintaining the poles directly in front of the student as they are completing the turn because of the pull of gravity and the student's heavy weight.

Overall, there are other disadvantages with poles when I compare to harnesses. They do not allow enough freedom for the child to ski on their own. Basically, with the pole methods, you are helping them to maintain the child's speed and doing some of their work with balance, and by assisting in the turning process. Ski harnesses can allow complete freedom of movement when you are not pulling on the reins.

Photo 34. A three-year-old girl holding on to one end of the coach's pole to maintain balance as she is guided around a turn.

Photo 35. A ski instructor is skiing backward with his ski poles extended out horizontally so that his student can grab onto it for speed control and assistance with turning.

Photo 36. A coach is skiing backward with his ski poles extended in front of him for assisting a child going down the hill.

Cones

These tools are used as markers to indicate where the directional changes should take place. Initially, you could space the cones with minimal change in turn direction, and to space them far apart so they have enough time to initiate the turns and complete the turns around the cones. Be respectful of the steepness of the slope when placing the cones. Speed is a detriment at this stage of their learning curve because it hinders their movements that are necessary to make linked turns. When cones are not readily available, use your ski poles or gloves to mark the spots on the hill. You can be creative and make your own markers, (e.g., Small flags, brightly-colored tennis balls that are cut in half, plastic lids, ribbons tied to sticks, paint brushes [paint the brushes with bright colors] turned upside down in the snow). Ski brushes of various sizes and color can be purchased (See photo 37). Simply telling the child to turn gets boring, non-challenging, routine, and not fun or exciting; Use props that they can see and interact with to ensure to have fun. I remember, while being trained by ex-Olympians out east at a younger age, how much fun racing was. I distinctly remembered waiting in the rice gate—how my heart raced—and how challenging it was making those turns around the gates at such high speeds on a steep terrain. In racing, you do not turn freely wherever and whenever you want; your turns and turn-shape are dictated by where the gates are placed on the race hill! So, it is a more disciplined and challenging activity than just randomly turning on the slopes.

So, in your attempts to becoming an outstanding coach, build fun games, use tools that will maximize your success on the slopes, and create many means of one-of-a-kind memories for the kids and parents to remember you by. For example, I like using small flags to set up a race course because racing I was uses all five of the fundamentals of skiing.

Photos 37. There are useful tools to teach different-sizes turns as seen this four-year-old doing small radius turns at the top of the hill and larger-radius turns at the bottom of the hill.

Bridge

Skiing under a bridge is one of the favorite games among children. It can be simply made by cutting a large plastic hoop and placing each end into the snow. I like this exercise because you can coach the kids to get smaller by flexing (Closing) their ankles and then getting taller by opening the ankles (Extending) and reaching for the sky. As the saying goes, "You always want to try and kill two birds with one stone." With skiing under the bridge, they not only have fun, but they are working on skills that will assist with their skiing.

Photo 38. Three-year-old girl flexing her ankles and bending from her waist to get shorter as she goes under the bridge.

Flying disc. These flying saucers come in various sizes and have been around for ages. Because of its light weight they can is a useful tool for teaching children. Children in beginner's lessons are generally not given poles until they are towards the end of the intermediate performance zone level to help prevent distractions. So, what do they do with their hands? Usually they have their hands everywhere except up and in front of them. This is where flying-discs plastic saucers can help occupy their hands and keep them in front for better balance. Dollar stores also have small plastic or rope wheels that I use because the kids can pretend that they are race-car drivers.

Photo 39. Four-year-old boy is using a flying disc to pretend that he is a race car driver, while unknowingly doing an important balancing skill by keeping his arms and hands up and forward.

 Understanding and utilizing the many tools and props will help enhance the fun games that you can use to achieve a faster learning curve for all your students.

CHAPTER 6

Developing a Strong Foundation—Adventures, Drills, and Games to be Used to Teach the Skills

The name of the game is to develop creative coaching and make your lessons exciting and fun. There are hundreds of ways to do that and I am certain you can add to this list of adventures, drills, and games.[2-5, 9, 12, 13, 14, 15, 33,34, 46, 47] Whenever you introduce fun games, remember, they should involve one of the skills. Be mindful, not all children can do all of these drills based on their PSIA CAP development; so modify accordingly. Since kids love to mimic what you do, make certain your demonstrations are spot on. I will list them by categories of primary skills involved. Depending on what performance zone the child may be in, do not expect that the child to be able to do all the specific drills listed; you need to use proper judgement. Many categories of listed activities overlap.

Edge Control

Boot arcs. Draw smiley faces and sad faces in the snow.

Duck walk. With the ski tips pointing outward and having contralateral edge pressure, the skis can grip the snow to move forward like in the herringbone walk.

Gloved-hand under the ski-tip test. This is an excellent way of determining how much edge pressure is being applied to the front of the ski by your student. This chapter, under case study 4, will provide more detailed information on this exercise.

Side stepping. Using corresponding edges, do side steps up the hill.

Outrigger turns. This is a great edging and pressure drill; discussed in greater detail in chapter 9, under "Advanced Zone".

Cowboy turns. One-legged and two-legged; this is a great edging and pressure drill; discussed in greater detail in chapter 9, under "Advanced Zone".

Feeler turns. This is a great drill to keep the upper body quiet while using the ankles, knees, and hips to articulate the turns with edge and pressure controls. This drill is discussed in greater detail in chapter 9, under "Advanced Zone".

Hockey stops. More counter-movement for greater edging and pressure control and more rotary; discussed in greater detail in chapter 9, under "Advanced Zone".

Side slipping. Great drill for edging and pressure control; the contralateral edges should increase the edge angle and pressure to stop, and release when you wish to slide down the hill. Lateral balance is also involved with this drill.

Skiing the side wall of a hill. This is a great drill to break the habit of a wedge skiing and moving on to parallel skiing. This task can be accomplished by racing to the top of the sidewall. One can only get to the top if the skis are in parallel and not in a wedge platform. I tell them that "the student that achieve the highest position on the sidewall, gets to be my platoon leader."

Big-toe turns. Getting inside edge and pressure by squashing the bug with the big toe.

Pinky-toe turns. Getting the outside edge and pressure by playing the piano with the pinky toes.

Playing the piano with the toes. This is a great drill for changing directions with linked-turns; combine both the big-toe turn and pinky turns at the same time.

Squashing the marshmallow with the big or little toes and the arches of the feet. Great homework and on-snow drill for edge and pressure control; place a marshmallow under the arches of a barefoot or under the center of boot, and push down with a pronation pressure.

Double-fisted turns. This is a great edging and pressure drill and to move the ankle and knees to move together the same amount, side to side; discussed in greater detail in chapter 9, under "Advanced Zone".

Upper/lower-body separation. Great for creating more edge angle; discussed in greater detail in chapter 9, under "Advanced Zone".

Scooter turns with the toe of the other feet off the snow. Since you can only ride one scooter at a time for each turn to the right and to the left, you need to hop on the scooter (Weight transfer) and moves the knees in the direction of the turns. This drill is discussed in greater detail in chapter 9, under "Advanced Zone". Also, see photo 10.

Long-leg/short-leg turns. This is a great drill for flexing and extension as well as for all four skills. This drill is discussed in greater detail in chapter 9, under "Advanced Zone".

Pressure Control

Grabbing for the stars. Great flexing/extension drill; extend and reach with both hands and pluck the stars out of the sky; come down by flexing and put them in your front pockets.

Shooting the basketball into the hoop. Great flexing/extension drill; extend and jump shoot the basketball with both hands and come back down and dribble the ball, by flexing your ankle, knees, hips.

Heavy foot/light foot. Great pressure drill; one foot is forcibly placed on the snow (Ski) and the other foot (Ski) is raised slightly off the ground. This drill can be extended for elephant walks, bicycle ride, long-leg/short-leg exercises.

Picking apples and putting them in the basket. With both hands forward in an athletic stand, the downhill hand reaches for an apple and pulls it down; place it in the basket strapped to the downhill boot—all the while skiing.

Squashing the bug. Good drill for edge pressure; place the insect under the big toes and bury it into the snow! The exterminator has now eliminated all those nasty bugs!).

Popcorn. Good flexing/extension static or dynamic exercise; pop, pop, pop—throwing your hands up in the air and also hopping each time the corn kernel pops!

Walking on hot rocks (Or hot sand). Good flexing/extension drill; ouch, ouch; the rocks/sand is hot and it is burning my barefoot—I'm hopping around like a crazy person.

Hopping like a Jack Rabbit. Good flexing/extension activity like the popcorn and walking on hot rocks/sand drill.

Pedaling the bicycle. Like the popcorn, elephant walks, hot rocks/sand, riding the bicycle— all great weight-transfer and balance drills (More on pedaling the bicycle in chapter 9, under "Advanced Zone").

Car shock absorbers. Great retraction exercise; ride over small bumps, making sure that the head is scraping the ceiling while the legs are retracting to absorb the bumps.

Jumping rope. Good flexing/extension activity like the popcorn and walking on hot rocks/sand drill.

Gloved-hand under the ski-tip test. This is an excellent way of how much edge pressure is being applied by your student. This is discussed in greater detail in chapter 6, under case-study 4; will provide more detailed information on this exercise.

Rotary Control

Wedge Christies. This is a great drill for balancing on the downhill ski while using rotary on the uphill ski. Try doing Wedge Christies while doing garlands; it becomes a real challenge. This drill is discussed in greater detail in chapter 9, under "Advanced Zone".

Garlands. Great drill for weight transfer and rotary; edging and pressure control is also involved. You can continue with the Wedge Christie exercises and fuse them into garlands.

Making bowties or hourglass figures. Great static rotary drills focusing on rotary leg movements with a pivot point under the arch; if there is too much snow to do the drill, place the ski pole on the ground and place the center of the boot over the butt end of the pole, and make bowties and hourglass figures with greater ease.

Windshield wipers. Great static drill for moving the toes outward to do herringbone walks and other maneuvers.

Pizza/French fries. These rotary movements need careful attention; be sure that the movements have leg rotation all the way up into the hip socket and pivot point is under the arch.

Fan-progression turns. Great for conquering fear by making progressive larger J-turns while in the fall line.

Wedge change-ups. Great rotary drills; like the Pizza/French fry movements, careful attention needs to be made to where the movements are originate.

Gliding wedge. Like wedge change-up, focus on the proper execution of the movements and focus on whether or not the COM is over the BOS.

Headlight turns. These are great drills to keep the hands forward and pointing in the direction of the turns (Also causes a slight counter-movement for easier turning because of the edge angle created and the slight twisting movement causes the skis to turn due to the unwinding process of the counter).

Pointing the toes in the direction of the turns. This is another version of twisting the feet into the direction of the turn.

Balance[46]

Athletic stance.[5, 46] This is a body position with a hip-wide foot stance, a flexing of the ankles to get the knees forward (About thirty degrees on the slant on the femur), hips forward over the center of the feet, with a spine angle of approximately thirty degrees, with the eyes looking straight ahead. The arms should also be forward (More on the arm position in chapter 9, under "Advanced Zone: Pole Touch"). See photo 13 in chapter 3 of a three-y-old girl with good balance mechanics. Also examine children in good balance (Photos 12, 13, 15, 18, 19, 26, 43, 50-52) and in poor balance (14, 16, 20, 21,33).

Pedal the canoe. In an athletic stance, reach forward towards the tip of the ski and pedal back to slightly behind the ski breaks while maintaining balance.

Hop turns. This activity was discussed in the A"ll four Skills" section.

Shuffle turns. This activity was discussed in the "All four Skills" section.

Riding the scooter. This is a great drill for weight transfer and balance, which is discussed in greater detail in chapter 9 under "School Drill".

Flamingo, crane, stork with one leg up. This is a great balancing drill on snow or for homework.

Flamingo drill: lifting one leg and balancing the other[46]

Thumpers. While balancing on the downhill ski, thump the uphill ski as one traverses the slope; reverse the drill by being balanced on the uphill ski and thumping on the downhill ski while traversing the hill.

Tap dancing. This is similar to the Thumper drill; just sing a bit...tap, tap, tap.

One thousand papers steps: Like the shuffle drill, the one thousand steps are a great drill to check if your body alignment is correct, especially when going through the turns. There should only be a smooth, continuous turn without hesitations. If hesitations occur, then the student is out of balance and is regrouping his COM to be over her BOS).

Fly like Superman or (Superwoman). With hands forward, check the child athletic stance while skiing.

Driving a race car. Like Superman or Superwoman drills, keeping the hands forward with a wheel, promotes proper balance.

Spearing the frog. Spearing a frog ahead of you or to the side of you require fore or lateral balance. Do not use this exercise while demonstrating pole touch. Stabbing the frog or salmon causes a delay in removing the ski pole tip from the snow and causes the downhill shoulder to open up, causing the skier to be out of balance.

Keeping a $100 dollar bill between the shin and tongue of the boot. This is a great exercise to promote shin-tongue contact at all times (See figure 18).

A child lost the $100 bill because he leaned back, causing the loss of shin contact with the tongue of the boot. This movement causes the lost of balance.[46]

Touch and turn. Pole touches are a timing device to gain rhythmic turns, a reminder to turn around the pole, creating a stable upper body with both legs and planted pole in the snow. More on the arm position and usefulness of pole touches in chapter 9, under "Advanced Zone", Pole Touch.

Knees ahead of the toes. Assist with flexing the ankles to get the COM forward.

Nose ahead the toes. Same with knees before the toes; it allows the knees, hips, and upper body to move forward.

Holding the serving tray (And serving the Queen of England tea). Keeps the hands forward and during the turns, causes a counter movement because the tray needs to be facing the Queen sitting in her throne at the bottom of the hill. Also, tell the students that the tray needs to be level; do not spill the tea!.

Butterfly wings. Flapping the wings promotes fore/aft and lateral balance.

Airplane wings. Tipping the wings into the turns causes the uphill hip, shoulders and arms to tilt upwards, while the downhill hip, shoulders, and arms to tilt downwards, causing a better body alignment for turns.

Jumps. Like hoping, it is a great flexing/extension exercise for pressure and balance control. See photo 40 below.

Photo 40. Three-year-old boys jumping on the markers placed on the snow to practice flexing and extending of the ankles for pressure control.[46]

Clapping their hands in front and back of them. Great static and dynamic drills for promoting balance; more advanced skiers can use a pole to pass from the front to the back while skiing.

Jumping. This is an excellent drill for practicing flexing and extending the ankles for pressure skills.

Balancing board. Any board with a hard ball underneath to challenge your balancing skills.

127

All Skills with Balance

Red light/green light. Can even add yellow light.

Ski like an animal. Fun games (Heavy elephant walks for pressure control, swimming fish for making many turns, walking penguin for weight-to-weight transfer, flamingo standing on one leg for fore/aft balance.)

Hand skiing. Visualization of what the skis are doing, tipping, neutral, tipping.

Follow the leader. Fun game.

Spreading the peanut butter and jelly. Skis intended to smear the snow from turn to turn.

Cat and Mouse. Fun chasing game.

Traffic cop or ski patrol. Fun stopping, chasing game.

Cops and Robbers. Fun chasing game.

Simon says. Fun game.

Synchro turns. Sophisticated turns that take a lot of timing, coordination, and synchronizing of the eyes and body to match everyone's turns.

S-Turns. For faster speed while making turns down the hill.

C-Turns. For medium-controlled speed down the slope.

J-Turns. For making a turn and coming to a stop.

Falling leaf. Like side slipping, it is a great drill for edging and pressure controls; it also utilizes lateral and fore/aft balance and a little bit of rotary control when pretending you a leaf falling to the ground.

Pivot slip. Uses all five fundamental skills of skiing.

Scavenger or treasure hunt. Entertainment and use of all skills.

Hockey stops. For making counter movements; great for edge angle control, pressure control, rotary control, and balance.

Skating. Great drill for all three skills and balance.

Pivot slips. Great drill for all three skill-control movements and balance.

360-degree turns on the snow. Fun and great drill for all three skills and balancing movements. Start out with a J-Turn, then shift the COM to the rear and swing both skis around until they point downhill.

Cones for Race Course. Fun and uses all three skills and balance.

Pivot Slips. Great drill for quick turns in narrow spaces; a full discussion is provided in chapter 9 in the Advanced Performance Zone.

Attack dove bomber. Tilting one wing into the turn, ankle, knees, hips moving uphill; body alignment and weight shift occurs.

Racing. Uses the Five Fundamental Skills of skiing.[29]

Hop turns. Flexing and extending the ankles, knees, and hips to hop up. Then, while coming down, flexing the ankles, knees, and hips, while using rotation into the turns and maintain balance.

Shuffle turns. This is a great exercise to check on proper alignment of the COS over the BOS throughout the turn. More is discussed in greater detail in chapter 9.

I will provide a few specific examples of what, when, how, and why you can use some of these maneuverers during your lessons.

Example: Case Study 1

Skating. Whenever I have time in a group lesson because I'm waiting for the entire class to show up for the lesson, I gather the student waiting on the flat ground to skate. I place two ski poles about twenty feet apart and tell them to skate around the poles, I make it fun and exciting by telling them that it is a race and the winner will be my ski patroller to lead the class. This drill of skating requires rotary, edging, pressure, and balance. Plus, this exercise blows off some steam and anxiety before the lesson.

Example: Case Study 2

Riding the scooter. This drill emphasizes importance of being balanced on one ski. When I do the flat-ground scooter exercises at the beginning of the lesson, I focus on their COM; if they are balanced, can they lift the other leg and glide down the gentle grade without falling (See photo 17 for proper body alignment on the skis). This preamble is followed by statement that you can only ride one scooter at a time. Thus, when the child is starting to make a turn, the scooter that they are ridding is the new uphill one, and the child will complete the turn on that one scooter. They need to "jump" (Weight transfer) on to the other scooter to start the next turn. This weight shift should be gradual and progressive. Static exercises such as pretending to be a stork, crane, or flamingo can help with balancing and weight transfer to one leg. Being in an athletic stance is paramount to achieve success with this drill. See photos 14 and 15 for a picture-perfect athletic stance and page for a description of the athletic stance (See figure 10).

Example: Case Study 3

Riding the bicycle. This is a great exercise to promote the long leg/short leg concept. Inform the student, "When you push one pedal down, what happens to the other pedal?" Can they visualize one leg getting long (As they push down on one pedal) and one leg getting short (As the other pedal goes up)? Also, tell them that the long leg is the heavy foot (More pressure) and the short leg is the light foot (Less pressure). If executed properly before the turn initiation, the body movements will allow the COM to cross the BOS towards the downhill skis—the up-hill leg should be longer for proper edging and pressure to occur. This longer leg allows the uphill ski to be on the inside edge because the longer leg is further away from the center line of the body, which creates more edge angle. The shorter leg (Ankle flexing) brings the skis closer to the body, which allows the ski to flatten, releases the snow, and allows gravity to pull the downhill ski tip into the turn. You can also actively rotate the leg to assist the skis to change direction. I want to caution you about using this riding the bicycle method with younger children because they may not have the cognitive or physical skills to execute the complex movements. A common fault that can occur is that the child is not balanced on the uphill ski, transfers too much weight to downhill skis, and hangs on in that position, which creates banking. I sometimes just simplify tell them, "You can just point your toes in the direction of the turns." Younger children may have more success with rotary to make turns than the more complex long leg/short leg movement. To help maintain their posture (Athletic stance) and balance on the skis, I also tell them, "We are skiing in a dark forest; always keep both headlights up and always point them in the direction of the turns." Whenever a person's arms and hands are down alongside their legs, they will be in the back seat of the skis. You also can tell them, "When your mom or dad drives the car, are they in the front seat or back seat? Well, you're driving those skis under you, and you better be in the front seat to control them. One of the ways of being forward is to keep your hand in front of you at all times while maintaining the Athletic Stance. Also, you need to push your shins forward by touching the tongue of the boot to remain forward at all times.

As an exercise, close your eyes and with your hands straight out directly in front of you; then, while focusing on the soles of your feet, what direction is the pressure on the soles of your feet moving as you drop your hands and arm to the side? This is a convincing exercise to discovering the importance of hand position during skiing. There are many nonbelievers about the importance of hand position; have them try this exercise to convert them!

Example: Case Study 4

Squashing the bug with the big toe and smashing the marshmallow with their arch. This gives them the feeling and mental vision of what it takes to get the skis on edge. I always tell my students that there are only two ways to turn those skis: "(1) pointing your toes in the direction of the turn (Rotation) or (2) using those edges with varying degrees of pressure throughout the turn." A great exercise to use is placing your gloved hands under the ski (Towards the front) and tell pretending they are turning on the new outside ski. Check for the amount of edging and pressure being applied. If you suspect it is not enough, check to see if the student's COM directly over the BOS, and if the child's shin pressing on the tongue of the boot. If the COM is behind the BOS, the child cannot get sufficient leverage to apply enough pressure. Acknowledge the laws of physics. People with longer legs have the added advantage of having their fulcrum at a higher spot to be able to use more body force to the skis (Or what often is said, "crushing the cuff of the boot"). So, the toddlers (And even shorter adults) will struggle more to get sufficient pressure versus people with longer legs. For future reference, this static exercise will be referred to as the gloved-hand Under the ski tip test. With time and experience, you will be able to tell how much edge pressure each age group and each performance zone group will be able to deliver.

Example: Case Study 5

Picking apples, or shooting the basketball. These games are fun to do, and the kids love executing them and other similar activities, like jumping rope and hopping around like a bunny rabbit. They promote flexing and extending while trying to maintain balance. With picking apples, your reach for the apple and place it into the downhill basket next to the downhill boot. With the basketball, you jump-shoot the ball in an extended position and come back down to regroup for the next jump shot. When a child is in a wedge, the edge angles (Contralateral edges) of both skis can be large, especially when the BOS is beyond hip width, which can make turn initiation more difficult than it should be. To help overcome that, reduce the size of the wedge and incorporate flexing and extending, which can flatten the edge angle to increase the ease of turn initiation. The downhill ski, in particular, needs to be in a neutral position for it to release and let gravity help move it in the direction of the new turn. Besides, being static is not good; you want dynamic movements involved to make more fluid and smoother turns, I always make it fun by saying, "You're not robots. Being stiff and upright when making your turns make other people on the hill think that you are R2-D2 in *Star Wars*.. I want you to show me that you're not just a mechanical machine but a real live person. Relax and have fun when making those nice, big turns."

Example: Case Study 6

Hop turns and shuffling throughout the turns. Theses activities are great for checking whether or not their COM is forward and whether their alignment is perpendicular to their skis (See figure 16) throughout the turns. If those two features are not correct, the child will not be balanced to execute the necessary turning skills. If the shuffle can be done continuously without stopping during any phase of the arc to ensure the kid is in balance. If you see hiccups or momentary stops in the shuffling, then the kid is trying to rebalance herself to continue shuffling. This exercise can be used with adults too, even experienced skiers.

So, in summary, there are many drills that you can use, but be certain that you select ones that are appropriate to teach the primary skill for that moment. I am sure that you can add to these lists of many activities that have worked for you.

 Knowing how to use the many different fun drills that specifically teach a movement skill will not only enhance the learning process but also motivate children to learn more about skiing. Be creative and innovative in your lesson plans to motivate and excite kids to ski better with fun.

CHAPTER 7

Developing a Strong Foundation—Special Behaviors and Challenges

Once in a great while, you may encounter an individual that does not fit the norm.[1] This can pose difficulties when trying to present a lesson to that child. They may be disorderly, inattentive, disinterested, disobedient, or out of character for that age group. It can be frustrating for you, as a dedicated coach, who wants to exceed customer satisfaction all the time. There are some special conditions that warrant a closer look. According to the US Census Bureau, the overall percentage of children with disabilities is around 14 percent. There are thousands of these special conditions I could write about, but I will focus on some of the most common encounters that I have observed on the hill. As a coach, you need to be aware, be able to spot these special individuals, and also be able to best handle them on the slopes. Here are some examples:

Cognitive Disorders[1]

A slow-learning child hits developmental markers at a much slower rate than his peers. It is commonly misunderstood that these children fail at learning or are merely "dumb". The truth is that every child has the child's own pace to learn and develop. Some children naturally learn much faster, while others are known to take their time to learn the same concepts and lessons. Mild cognitive impairment is a frequent observation. A child with specific learning disability is one of average or above average intelligence but has specific limitations, such as reading, writing, hearing, or seeing, which can make learning very difficult. There may be defects in any of the basic central nervous system (CNS) functions, which have to do with listening, speaking, reading, and writing. The CNS may also be directly involved in the brain, where thinking, memory, and reasoning take place.

Here are some coaching tips to assist you with these special groups of individuals:

- To cope with these special people, adjust your expectations and specific goals. Keep their goals smaller to gain success.
- Exercise more patience and tolerance.
- Never raise your voice—tone is important.
- Reward them with unlimited praises.
- Ask the child's parent, "Is there is anything I need to know about your child?"

Attention Deficit Disorder (ADD)/Attention Deficit Hyperactivity Disorder (ADHD)[1]

ADD is a common behavioral disorder, in which someone has problems with learning and may have a behavior problem because they cannot think about or pay attention to things for long periods. These individuals are extremely active, act impulsively, and can be easily agitated. They may daydream a lot, can be easily distracted, can forget things more than most, and struggle with sitting still.

ADHD is a form of ADD, and is the result of decreased right-brain activity, which regulates social behavior, impulsivity, and attention. There are three different types of ADHD:

Inattentive type. These kids struggle to focus on tasks and activities.

Hyperactive-impulsive type. These children struggle with the constant need to be active and tend to act without thinking.

Combined type. These individuals struggle with inattention, hyperactivity and impulsivity.

Here are some common characteristics of ADHD and ADD:

- is easily distracted
- does not seem to listen when spoken to directly
- fidgets, seems restless
- often loses things that are necessary for tasks (Their belongings, where they put their equipment)
- interrupts or intrudes on others
- blurts out answers
- difficulty waiting their turn

- complains of normal things, like being "bored"

Here are some coaching tips that you can use on and off the hill to manage ADD children:

- Most have normal to above-normal intelligence; so do not "talk down" to them.
- Keep the routine. The process needs to be the same each time; repeat the instructions in a calm, positive matter, if needed. They do not handle changes well, so try to avoid transitions and physical relocation.
- When communicating, always use direct eye contact, and have a calm attitude and voice.
- Use visual cues like drawing in the snow. Use props, puppets, stuffed animals, and surrounding pictures and photos.
- Your lesson plans need to be *active*. You need to *move* and avoid being *stagnant* and boring.
- Be creative; children with ADD are easily frustrated and stressed, and fatigue can break down their self-control and lead to poor behaviors.
- Check for understanding; if you failed, take another approach.
- Use terrain as a tool. It can be an alternative to verbal communication. It can help alleviate the challenges that arise as a result of frustrations, inability to communicate needs, or simply sensory overload.
- Always ask the parent, "Is there anything special that I need to know about your child?"

Autism[1]

Autism Spectrum Disorder (ASD) is a complex neurological disorder characterized by a spectrum of developmental disorders that can range from a lack of social interaction, lack of communication, repetitive behaviors, or special interests and talents. Often times, these spectra of disorders can be characterized by impaired communication, extreme self-absorption, detached from reality, destructive behavior, and resistance of physical or eye contact. Every autistic child has their own distinctive fingerprint; no two children with this disorder are alike. Thus, their behaviors can be widely different from one child to the next. Some autistic kids have especially high abilities for numbers, music, and other unique features. There are four basic types of autistic kids at the ski resorts, and we tend to see the mildest form, known as Asperger's Syndrome. I will only discuss this form, which is characterized by impaired social skills and by the lack of physical coordination.

Here are some teaching tips to use:

- Try not to make body or eye contact.
- Stay away from loud noises like the blowing snow guns and large, noisy crowds.
- Be creative.
- Keep tasks simple and repetitive.
- Speak slowly and clearly.
- Pay attention to what pleases and what annoys the child.
- Do not treat them as difficult, uncommunicative, dysfunctional person, but a very special person with special needs.
- Check with the parent to learn previous routines that the child liked; communication style, learning style; and how to deal with tantrums and reward systems.
- Look for other special signs like being aware that a child likes numbers. I once had a six-year -old boy that always informed me what number chair we were sitting on; he was 100 percent correct every time!

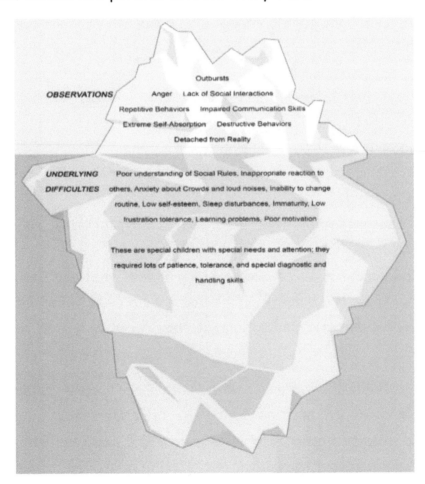

Figure 15. Iceberg Model: ASD's obvious obervations (Above the water) and the less obvious and sometimes hidden difficulties (Below the water)[1]

Diabetes[1,53]

I decided to include this disease because it is so common; in fact, there is an epidemic in our American society today, with no clear indication that it will end soon. Over 70 percent of our children are overweight and obese, resulting in a steep and rapid rise in diabetes (Close to 45 percent), and with type-2 diabetes being six times more prevalent than type-1 diabetes. Those with this endocrinologic disease cannot properly process sugars. There are Three types of diabetes:

Type-1 Diabetes. The disease starts very early in childhood. The pancreatic cells have been destroyed by the immune system; thus, it cannot produce enough insulin, which is needed to carry the sugar into the cells for energy. These individuals require exogenous insulin to maintain their carbohydrate metabolism. Too much exogenous insulin results in the blood sugar to rapidly drop (Usually within a few seconds to a few minutes). This hypoglycemic condition can result in loss of cognitive function and the child may go into comma or even death. Lesser symptoms include fatigue, irritability, loss of attention and even cognition, being jittery, sweaty, or thirsty.

What can you do?

- Recognize the hypoglycemic symptoms.
- Stop what you are doing and immediately take the child to the parent or the ski patrol hut.
- Provide sugar if you are certain that it is a hypoglycemic reaction and not a hyperglycemic reaction.
- Ask the parent if there are anything special that you should know about Johnny. If he is a diabetic, if he had a good meal before of the lesson, if he took his diabetic medications, if they recently tested the child's blood sugar?

Type-2 Diabetes. While this form of diabetes can occur in early childhood, it is more common later in childhood, such as during the teen years and in adulthood, when overweight and obesity become more rampant. The pancreas still produces the normal amount of insulin, but the body is resistant to it, and the insulin cannot attach to the receptor sites on the cell. This inhibits the insulin-carrying sugar from getting into the cell. The pancreas tries to produce more insulin (Overproduction) in an attempt to correct the situation. Hyperinsulinemia results, causing many other metabolic problems. Common symptoms include being thirsty, hungry, tired, blurred vision, sweating, irritability, cognitive impairment and frequent urination. The symptoms of high blood sugar (Hyperglycemia) are very similar to hypoglycemia. While both conditions are important to recognize, hypoglycemia is the more important one to focus on when on the hill. You can ask the child:

When did you last eat,

What did you eat,

Did you take your medication?

Are you carrying a glucometer?

The blood sugar status of the child is dependent on (1) Insulin, (2) the amount, kind, and timing of the food intake, and (3) duration, intensity, and frequency of the physical activity (See figure 14) and the amount of insulin or other glucose-lowering medication taken. Any time the child shifts one of the components in the triangle, (e.g., Increasing the amount of physical activity, such as skiing, or not eating the usual diet, the sugar metabolism will be out of control, resulting in the symptoms described above.

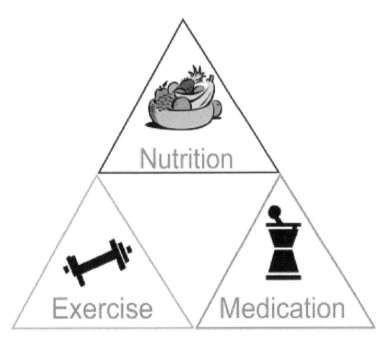

Figure 16. Diabetes Triad

What can you, as a coach, do to assist in a hypoglycemic crisis, which is similar to what is listed above under type-1 diabetes?

The main thing to acknowledge about diabetes is when the child's blood sugar is out of control, especially during hypoglycemia. You must work quickly because the level of cognitive confusion occurs within a few seconds to minutes. Unconsciousness and even death may occur.

Gestational diabetes. This form occurs in pregnancy. Since this type does not apply to the children we teach, I will not expand this discussion.

Developmental disability.[1] These conditions result from congenital abnormalities, trauma, disease, or deprivation, which interrupts or delays normal fetal, infantile, or juvenile growth and development. Some common developmental disabilities include intellectual disability (Slower learner, mental retardation, Down's syndrome), neurological development (Multiple myeloma, balance impairments, cerebral palsy), and other emotional behavior disabilities. I have touched on the slow learner. Now I will cover another common disorder, Down's syndrome.

Down's syndrome.[1] These special kids generally enroll in the adaptive programs with certified adaptive staff, which are available at various ski resorts. We are beginning to see more students with Down's syndrome at the regular snow sports programs and in the private lessons. This is a genetic disorder in which there are three no.21 chromosomes. This trait can be passed on by either parent. There are over six thousand babies born every year with this syndrome. The facial appearances, intellectual disability, and developmental delays are characteristic of this disorder. The clinical features are as follows:

- Eyes are shaped like almonds.
- The face is flatter, especially the nose; small ears, that may fold over a bit at the top.
- Tongue tends to stick out of their mouth.
- They may have small hands, fingers, and feet.
- They may have low muscle tone and strength.
- They may have loose joints, making them very flexible.
- They may have short height, neck.
- They may have small head.

- They may have mild to moderate cognitive capacities; their ability to think, reason, understand and socialize may be compromised.
- Behavioral problems may exist, such as not being able to pay attention well, obsessiveness about some things. They have a harder time to control their impulses, relate to others, and manage their feelings when they get frustrated or stressed.
- They are more likely to have hearing losses, visual problems, heart and endocrine (Especially the thyroid gland) issues.
- Keep the teaching simple and minimize frustrating circumstances or introducing stressful tasks and drills; follow the KISS Principle; stick to the same way each time you practice the same tasks and drills for these children with disabilities.
- Kids with Down syndrome are very social and they love affection. Sometimes they will misbehave because of some underlying reason that you may have created; provide lots of positive reinforcement to build their self-esteem and confidence. Hugs go a long way with this group.
- Be sure communicate with their parents. You may receive tips on what works (e.g., Being consistent, being patient, focusing on long-term goals). Their behavior is a way of communicating.
- Change your attitude and coaching approach; use the same ideas but modify the way you deliver the message.
- Rewards are important for these kids. I have more than over three dozen sheets of stickers that they can pick from after the lesson to place on their helmet.
- Pick your battles; is the behavior dangerous or just bothersome?
- Avoid power struggles by giving them choices or alternative pathways to accomplish the same objectives.
- Make the harder tasks and drills more fun. Make it less challenging and offer toys to have fun and take away the stigma that tasks are too difficult.
- With dangerous behaviors, the child needs structure and boundaries. Having time-out periods can be handy.
- Redirecting your approach and providing choices are paramount to successfully coaching to these unique students.

Let me share with you another story about a child with a slight disability. Lev was a seven-year-old boy who came out to ski for the first time. It was a beautiful sunny day, and I had a brief discussion with him and his dad to obtain their goals and to try and develop a student's profile. The dad said, "He is super excited and he talked about it for two weeks with his friends."

Lev didn't say much; I gathered he was a little bashful and was on the quiet side. He was slightly tall and slender for his age. As we proceeded with the one-hour lesson, it became apparent that he struggled doing side steps up the short four-foot runoff hill. I told Lev, "I will help him carry his skis up the hill, and he can put the downhill ski on first, followed by the uphill ski."

I soon found out that he could not push his boots into either binding; I had to help him push each boot into each binding. I had to do this procedure all lesson long. Also, he had difficulty completing his C-turns in either directional changes. By this time, I was able to assess Lev and decided that this cognitive development was an 11, his affective development was a 9, and his physical development was a 7. I decided to use a harness to guide him down the hill as we went higher onto the slope. When we were finished with the lesson, I asked Lev if he had fun, and he said, "Yeah, big time, Coach Pineapple Herb!"

I asked his dad if there was something that I should know about his precious son.

He said, "Yes, I forgot to tell you that he had a slight case of muscular dysfunction, which required him to take physical therapy. I apologize."

I said there was absolutely no problem. I was booked for the rest of the season with Lev. By the end of our short season, Lev was able to make C-wedge turns on an intermediate hill with some assistance with the ski harness. His assigned homework was pressure control by doing hops (Extension and flexing) for five minutes every day. His reward for the lesson was his favorite: a chocolate candy bar (With the approval of his father). His Dad was beside himself. I have never seen so much enthusiasm and excitement between the father and the child with his skiing performance and his new love for the sport. The morale of the story is follow the triple-A rule. At all times when you have a customer,

- Be Aware
- Be Alert, and
- Be Attentive

You'll never know what to expect with your clients, so follow the motto: "Always, be prepared."

Special kids need special attention; know their unique medical conditions and know how to deal with them, and adjust your teaching style to adapt to these special people.

CHAPTER 8

Developing a Strong Foundation—Teaching by Age Group

Kids learn at different paces at different ages. They can only execute what they can understand and process the amount and kind of information based on their cognitive, emotional, and physical developments. When developing your lesson plans, be spot-on with your assignment; for the most part, you do not have a second chance. Don't run into a brick wall and say, "I coulda, I woulda, I shoulda." This is game time; there is no plan B for your A Game! In this chapter, I will provide information of specific age groups using the PSIA CAP model[2-5,13,14,33,46] which was introduced in chapter 1, fig. 2. I will go into greater depth for each age group. For convenience, the three age groups I cover are: (1) three- to six-year old (tiny tots), (2) seven- to ten-year old, and (3) eleven- to eighteen-plus-year-old.

The Three- to Six-Year-Old Age Group

Cognitive. Jean Piaget was a Swiss psychologist; his theory on kids suggests that children progress through a series of four different stages of cognitive development. These stages encompass numerous aspects of mental development, including reasoning, language, morals, and memory. He believed that kids take an active role in this cognitive development, building knowledge as they interact with their immediate world surrounding them.

In this age group, they do not yet understand concrete logic, cannot mentally manipulate information, and are unable to take the point of view of other people. According to Piaget, these are the sensory-motor stage and pre-operational phase. Children become increasingly adept at using symbols, as evidenced by increases in playing and pretending. For example, a child is able to use an object to represent something else, such as pretending that a stuffed monkey is a real monkey riding on the child's back. With this group, role-playing also becomes important. Kids may play the role of a policeman, a robber, superman, superwoman, a dive bomber, or a rabbit hopping around.

Kids in this age group are egocentric. If you ask the kid to describe a dog, they will use what they saw on TV or their own dog, if they have one. They do not have the know-how to describe what another person's perspective might be. Many developmental psychologists refer to the ability to understand that other people have different perspectives, thoughts, feelings, and mental states, as in theory of mind. To put this into perspective, if equal amounts of liquid are poured into two identical containers and the liquid in one container is then poured into a differently shaped cup—such as one tall, and thin cup and the other into a short, wide cup—which do you think the child in this age group will select when asked which cup holds the most liquid? Despite seeing that the liquid amounts were equal, they will almost always choose the cup that appears fuller.

Piaget found that few kids showed any understanding of conversation prior to the age of five. In summary, they lack the understanding that things look different to other people and that objects can change in appearance while still maintaining the same properties.

He also found that at this stage, the tendency is to focus on only one aspect of a situation at a time (Centration). For example, try lining up to two rows of paper clips in such a way that a row of five paper clips is longer than a row of seven paper clips. Ask the child to point to the row that has more paper clips, and the child will point to the row of five. This is because children at this age focus on one aspect (Length only) and cannot manipulate two (Length and number). As kids get older, they'll develop the ability to decenter.

Children at this stage of development play alongside other children but not with them. Don't worry. This does not imply that the little one is antisocial; it simply means that the child is absorbed in their own world. At this stage, children move from parallel playing to including other children in games. That's when "let's pretend" games work best. So, coaches, a tip or Advice, keep the conversation simple. Use words and graphics that match their level of understanding!

There are six sensorimotor stages: (1) reflexes, which occurs between ages zero to four months; the child understands the environment purely through inborn reflexes, such as sucking and looking; (2) primary circular reactions; during this substage (4-8 months), the child becomes more focused on the world and begins to intentionally repeat an action to trigger a response in the environment, like crying or screaming aloud; (3) coordination of reactions during this substage (8-12 months), clearly intentional actions take place. Children will often begin exploring the environment around them and imitate the observed behaviors of others. The understanding of objects also begins during this time, and they begin to recognize that certain objects have specific qualities. For example, a rattle will make a sound when shaken; (4) tertiary circular reactions; during this substage (12-18 months), this is the period of trial-and-error experimentation. For example, the child will try out different sounds or actions as a way of getting attention from the parent; (5) early representational thought; at this substage (18-24 months), children begin to develop symbols to represent events or objects in the world. They move towards understanding the world through mental operation rather than purely through instinct and reactions; (6) object permanence is one of the most important accomplishments at this sensorimotor stage of development. The child's understanding is now extended to knowing that objects continue to exists even though they cannot be seen or heard. For example, image a game of peek-a-boo; a very young child will believe that the other person or object has actually vanished and will act shocked or startled with the object reappears.

The pre-operational stage talking begins around age two and lasts until seven, where symbolic play and learning to manipulate symbols occur. Language development is one of the hallmarks of this period. During this stage, children begin to engage in make-believe scenarios.

Affective. At this developmental stage, children begin to understand right from wrong. Kids like to acknowledge adults as all-knowing and always doing the right thing. They respect authority as their leaders in their world. They certainly respect police officer, a captain in the military, a teacher, a coach, and their parents. Structure in a kids' life begins now. Their moral compass begins now. Boy and girls alike can display a wide range of emotions at this stage of growth. That is why I sometimes experience both genders to be high-strung and react with high degrees of emotions, depending on the scenario. Children who attend Pre-school have an added advantage over those who do not when it comes to communication and socializing with other children.

Physical. At this developmental stage, the COM is higher due to body-to-head ratio, which tends to place the COM behind the BOS. Children at this stage develop from top to bottom, and form the core of the body outward to the extremities. The neuromuscular coordination and muscle development are less refined. The large muscles are preferred over the smaller muscles for movements. Many of the physical movements are governed by the genetic background of the child, by extracurricular experiences, and preparatory educational background. For instance, if a child has the luxury of attending dance classes or gymnastic classes, have older brothers or sisters or friends that they play a lot of outdoor games, or have parents that are athletically inclined, have better physical development and coordination. The brain is the control center and will fire the impulses down certain neurological pathways for the muscles to respond. The more they use the pathways, the more developed they become. That's why a quarterback has specific drills for the arms and hands and a running back has specific drills for their leg coordination and movements. We should do the same with each skill, by having specific drills to emphasize the brain-muscle coordinating specific movements.

Be aware that some toddlers may have difficulty turning because of the lack of coordination and strength. Your objective when making pizza turns is to get one ski edge to engage in the snow and the other ski to flatten out to release the contralateral edge from the snow. A great exercise to use is the child placing her hands on her knees and push the knees into the direction of the turns (See photo 34), which can meet your objective for turning. Be sure that the child moves both hands diagonally at the same time while keeping the knees the same distance from each other throughout the turn. Often times you will see a girl rather than a boy creating an A-frame by having one knee almost touching the other knee. Another advantage of using this technique is that it helps keep their weight forward because proportionally, their head is larger than the rest of the body.

Photo 41. A three-year-old girl is placing her hands on the kneecaps to assist in turns.

I like giving homework, whereby they do drills, like pretending to be a stork, crane, or flamingo, by balancing on one leg while lifting other. For the summer, I tell the parents to invest in a 4' x 4' x 8' post and a 2' x 4' by 8' post. Cut the later post in half and nail each half to each end of the first post to add stability. That will be their child's high beam. It will be a great balancing exercise, similar to what gymnast do for practice (See photograph 5 in chapter 1).

Because the neuromuscular muscular coordination and strength develops from top to bottom and from the core outward with this age group, you may want to do foot drills in the snow. Children generally have fun doing the drills if you yourself participate. In addition, they can mimic the movements that you do.

Photo 42. Children and their coaches sitting in the snow doing foot drills (Making pizzas and French fries).

Photo 43. This is a fun game to do because the children and coaches are lifting one leg as they see how long they can maintain their balance on the other leg.[46]

One of the more difficult tasks for a child in this age group to do is the side steps on the snow. This is especially true if the snow texture is mushy or slick like a sheet of ice. You might want to suggest to your ski school to build an inclining ramp with carpet on the surface for indoors activities. You can assist the child climbing up the ramp sideways, all the while coaching the body movements that are necessary to do the side steps properly.

Photo 44. A three-year-old boy being assisted by his coach as he learns the side steps on the ramp.

What can you expect as realistic goals for a three- to six-year-old age group? For their first lesson or two, considering the norm you can expect:

For a one-hour lesson, the child should be able to do foot drills (Pizza, French Fries, Duck walks (Toes pointing outward).

The child can draw smiley faces and sad faces with their boots in the snow.

The child can squash the bug with the big toes and pinky toes to get edging and pressure skills.

The child can squash the marshmallows when placed under the arch and big toes for edging and pressure drills.

The child can make bowties when pivoting under their arches for rotational movements.

The child can walk sideways like a crab or like a duck that walks up a slightly graded hill with the toes pointed outward and knees pointed inward to allow the inner edge of each ski to grab the snow.

Do a straight run on a slight-graded hill.

Do a gliding-wedge run with slight directional changes.

Come to a pizza stop, making sure that the BOS is not too much beyond hip width and using more ski-edge angle by pointing both their knees inward; both hands (One on the lateral side of each knee) can assist to push the knees inward if initially the children cannot master that movement.

They should be able to do scooter turns (Weight transfer to one scooter).

With subsequent lessons, they should be able to do linked C-turns on the beginner hill and be able to load, ride, and unload the people-mover carpet safely.

They can attempt to do the side-step and herringbone-step walks up a low-grade slope.

They can learn one of the four ways to get up after falling in the snow. After a fall, a common way to get up is by rolling over into a prone position while facing uphill and pushing backward until the child is upright. Children at this age are nimble and flexible and generally can do this exercise with ease. If the child is having difficulty getting up by themselves, give them a hand by pulling them up, ideally with the skis pointing perpendicular to the fall line and you're uphill and the student is below you.

Make sure that the student knows how to properly buckle their own boots; most beginners do not know. If they're too young, educate their parents. Inform them that the boots should fit snugly like a firm hand shake, just short of pain. Most of the time, beginning students buckle their boots to fit like bedroom sleepers for comfort.

Photo 45. A four-year-old girl is getting up after a fall by rolling over onto a prone position and pushing herself backward to get upright'

They should carry their own skis properly and safely from the lodge to the hill and back (See photo 46). I have observed skiers carrying their skis on their shoulders, which can cause an accident by hitting another person when they suddenly turn around. I tell the students to extend their arms out and carry their skis as if they are carrying a baby.

Photo 46. A three-year-old munchkin is carrying her own skis properly and safely.

Coaching Tips. So, what do you do with all this information as a coach? Here are some suggestions for this three- to six-year old age group:

"Always be prepared; expect the unexpected."

Never assume things. For example, don't assume all children at this age group know right from left. They seem to know colors better than directional changes. You can place a red dot on their right glove (For Right turns) and a lavender dot on the left glove (For left turns). If no self-sticking dots are available, you can cut 12" long red and lavender ribbons and tie them on their wrists. Believe it or not, I have actually taught 7- and 8-year-old students who didn't know their left from the right!

Give *one* direction at a time when providing instructions.

Keep the language simple, at a cognitive level that they can understand.

Keep it short and change the tasks often.

Make it exciting and *fun*; use your creative juices and imagination.[5, 46]

Introduce a lot of games they can identify with from previous experiences that will teach specific skills.

Reinforce successful tasks, and give tons of praises to these tiny tots.

Keep your students safe throughout the lesson by explaining lucidly what you mean, and check for understanding by playing roles.

Choose the terrain wisely and communicate to them the consequences when wrong choices are made; be aware of their abilities and what too steep a hill can do.

Check the size of their Pizza, turn shape, length of time the child is in the fall line (to regulate speed).

Try to understand the child's background and interests; use drills with other sports that use the same movement patterns.

Communicate at a voice level that they know you are caring, loving, and kind, never using a high level or screaming at them.

Analyze their behavior. What makes them tick? What opens their inner self to you and the world?

What is the child's motivation?

What is the child's CAP strengths and weaknesses for that age?

Are there any medical issues or handicaps?

Have their hierarchy of needs being met?[13,16,28,48]

Have you determined who is the customer and who is the consumer?

Do they have the proper ski gear?

Do the kids have any special needs?[1]

Do you have all the tools necessary to conduct a safe and fun lesson?

What are the expectations and goals of the parent and child. Are they idealistic or realistic?[5,16]

Are the goals for each task, movement, or topic realistic and not idealistic?[7,13]

Did you check the weather conditions for that day, that morning, that afternoon, that hour?

Did you teach any of the safety rules?

Do you have a backup plan for failures?

Bag of tricks. I will provide a short list of games and drills that work for this age group:

- Riding the scooter (Balancing on one leg).
- Ridding the bike (Long leg/short leg; weight transfer).
- Making arrows with the feet (Boots); big arrowheads will make you stop (Different degrees of edge angle).
- Pretending to be a stork, crane, or flamingo by standing on one leg and lifting the other (Balance).
- Shuffle across the terrain (Body alignment and balance).
- Bunny hops across while traversing or during a gliding wedge or straight run (Flexing and extending, pressure).
- Pointing both headlight in the direction of the turn (Counter-rotation).
- Making different shaped turns (Speed control).
- Making different size Pizzas (Speed control). Two major factors, heights and speed, can cause FEARS[16]. Let's focus on speed control[5], which can be managed by the:

(1) Proper selection of terrain steepness,
(2) Turn shape,
(3) Size of the wedge,
(4) How long the child remains in the fall line,
(5) If the child is parallel skiing; if so, to use less edge angle to allow skidding to slow down
(6) If the student has lost the child's balance and is out of control,
(7) Number of turns (More turns means slower speed,

154

(8) If you use special ski tools to control speed (Plastic hoops, ski harnesses, poles, and ski-tip connectors).

Figure 17. Different size-wedges and parallel platforms affects speed.

- Squashing the Bug (Edge and pressure control).
- Using toys such as a fuzzy chick, small stuffed animal, small steering wheel, or flying plastic disc to help occupy their hands and to keep them forward (Balance).
- Hopping around like crazy jack rabbits while in their boots (Flexing and extending, pressure).
- Seeing who can jump the highest in one place (Flexing and extending, increasing and decreasing pressure)?
- Putting stickers on the gloves to help understand right turns (Red dot) from left turns (Lavender dot).
- Placing a $100 bill (I use green paper money) between the tongue of the boot and shin of each boot, aka *shin-tung* philosophy in the Chinese culture (Balance).

When they lean back, the $100 will fly out of the boot. If they lose the $100, I tell them that they need to pay it back to me.

Figure 18. A child lost the $100 bill because he leaned back, causing the loss of the shin contact with the tongue of the boot. This unwanted movement caused the loss of balance[46]

- Walking to and from the ski hill (Coordination and balance).
- Provide opportunities for mileage: practice, practice, practice.
- Getting their attention by stimulating their curiosity. At this age, kids are very curious; try using a hand puppet or finger puppet. I always carry one in my pocket and use it when we're on the chairlift riding up. I have an animated discussion with whispers in my ear. This trick always works, especially for this age group! The child always reacts by saying, "What did Mojo say? Please tell me, please." I will respond by saying, "Well, he wants you to slow down by making big, fat C-turns." I get their attention, and they try to obey.
- Using Captain Zembo's secret recipe[9] for coaches for fun and imagination.[9]
- Recommend to the parent not to book a lesson around the child's nap time. You can be sure that there will be less motivation, less attentiveness, and less energy during that period. I actually had a 3-year-old fall asleep on me while riding the chairlift!

The seven- to ten-year-Old Age Group

Cognitive. In this age group of the preoperational stage, the development of the brain is more refined. Children demonstrate more independence, self-awareness, and self-confidence.

Their vocabulary increases to approximately two thousand words. They can compose sentences with five or more words. They can count up to ten objects at one time. They know left from right. They begin to reason, argue, and understand concepts like, yesterday, today, and tomorrow. They begin to use words like "why" and "because". They can copy complex shapes, such as drawing a diamond, a horse, a bird, or a snake. They have more vivid imaginations and can act out the role more realistically. They have a longer attention span and are willing to take on more responsibility. Kids at this age group can tell time, money, days of the week, and read articles of interest. This is the age group that can pretend to be Superman or Superwoman to help keep their hands forward.

Affective. Children at this age are somewhat innocent and trusting. They believe in law and order. According to their perspective, you are still the authority, but they may have little respect for your intelligence. They may challenge you with some comments when they think they know more about. The kids believe in their own cleverness and may disobey adult rules. They are more communicative and more socially inclined to spend more time with other kids. They are willing to share their toys and belongings with others. They are more willing to accept the opinions of others. They have the courage to question your thoughts and commands. They pay more attention to friendships and teamwork. They want to be liked and accepted by friends. They are better at describing their feelings. They begin to feel objects can have feelings. Their emotional swings can be greater; tempers can flair, crying can be endless, and joyous experiences can be off the charts. Children at this age are beginning to compare themselves to other people's expectations. They love to mimic others; thus, perfect and accurate demonstrations of movements on the slopes are a must.

Physical. At this age, the COM is slightly lower. Their motor movements are more refined, and their coordination of movements is smoother. They can begin to coordinate one half of the body with the other half with greater ease. Their physical strength and muscle reflexes are advancing. Their range of motion with their extremities shows better coordination and have an extended range.

Boys and girls develop differently; in general, both genders grow in height and weight at the same slow but steady rate. It is only later (Beyond ten years old) when the girls start to grow taller faster, although boys catch and exceed them within a few years.

What can you expect as realistic goals for a seven- to ten-year-old age group? For the first lesson or two, considering the norm you can anticipate the following:

- Everything that was stated for The three- to six-year-old student.
- Side stepping and duck walking on steeper hills for longer periods.
- Making larger directional movements in a wedge; ability to make J-turns to come to a stop and being able to make C-turns to slow down to initiate a new turn.
- Longer runs on the slopes and even linking some of the C-turns.
- With subsequent lessons, ability to load, ride, and unload the people mover or conveyer carpet and chairlift safely; ability to do linked C-turns on the majority of the beginner hill.
- Ability to get up three of the four ways.
- Different ways to control speed.

Coaching Tips. Here are some strategies that can help you:

- Give more than one direction at a time, but keep it simple and easy to understand.
- Use characters and themes that are appropriate for the lesson.
- They may be able to walk backwards, but they may not be able to comprehend a demonstration when you face them. So, face the same direction (While directly in front of them) when explaining a demonstration.
- Use imagination in your teaching, and do a lot of fun thing as you clown around on the hill. Many times, the kid will remember more about the fun things that you did than the ski lesson.
- Use as many props as you can to excite them and create a truly fun, safe, learning experience.

- Ask questions—they now have an expanded cognitive function, and these questions provide the opportunity to check for understanding.
- Kids in this age group are inquisitive. Ask them what and how they feel about a given topic.
- Build their self-esteem and confidence by giving positive feedback, praises, and high-fives.
- While their vocabulary has expanded, still keep it simple. Follow the KISS principle.
- Draw in the snow when explaining more complicated movements or subject matters, especially if they have a watcher learning style.
- They love learning at this age so, keep it interesting and challenging.
- They are very competitive; introduce a lot of games that are competition oriented in nature, whether they are competing with themselves or with others.
- Make them partners—ask them how, where, and when they want to try a new task or activity.
- They love to explore—challenge them with new ideas, new movements, and new terrain. Have a treasure hunt!
- You ask for feedback. At this age, kids are very candid and can be blunt. This will help you with your future lesson plans.
- Lighten up. Don't be so serious. Kids are there to have fun, not to attend a drill camp.
- Ensure your goals are realistic[46] and not idealistic[16,46] to ensure success and exceed customer satisfaction[7,13].

Bag of tricks. I will provide a short list of games and drills that work for this age group:

- Walking like a duck up the hill, or herringbone walk (All three skills and balance).
- Skating from one point to another (All three skills and balance[46]).
- Red light/Green Light (Edging and pressure).
- Stomping snow snakes through the turns (Pressure).
- Cops and robbers (All three skills and balance).
- Pointing the toes in the direction of the turns (Rotary control).
- Squashing the bug or marshmallow (Edging and pressure controls).

- Shooting the basketball (Flexing and extension, pressure control).
- Hopping like a rabbit (Flexing and extension, pressure control and balance).
- Turning like a dive bomber (Edging and pressure controls and balance).
- Setting up a race course (Using all Five Fundamentals of Skiing).
- Having a large stuffed animal on the kid's back (Balance).
- Magic tricks (Entertainment and bonding).
- Using puppets (Fun and entertainment).
- Wearing costumes or different types of hats to pretend you are a certain character (Fun and entertainment).
- They will view you as their friend, and not as an authoritative coach.
- Singing along with an artistic music-loving student (Entertainment and stress reduction).
- Finding what is current on kid's TV shows and mimicking their favorite star (Fun and entertainment).
- Pretending to throw passes to their favorite football star (Fun and entertainment)?
- Making small pizzas instead of large pizzas to make the turns easier (Edge control).
- Being a butterfly and flapping the wings (Lateral balance).
- Pretending they are ice cream sundae and you're pouring hot fudge at the top while they're imagining it is flowing slowly down the sides of the ice cream (Smooth movements).
- Jumping rope in one place (Flexing and extension, pressure controls).
- Unlike The three- to six-year-old group, the seven- to ten-year-old group love to explore and are very inquisitive. This is the age group that you need to focus on *"igniting the fire of curiosity."*
- Opportunities for mileage: practice, practice, practice.
- Homework to better prepare them for the next lesson.

Ages Eleven- to Eighteen- Years-Old

Cognitive. This is the beginning of the concrete operational phase, where the children begin to interact with the world around them verbally, mentally, and physically. The mental process is more sophisticated; logic and reasoning are more predominant in the thinking process. For example, if there are two rows of pennies but one row is spread out further apart, they know that the same number of pennies exist in both rows. With the teens, the information travels faster through the brain and nervous system, resulting in quicker movements and better coordination. By the time they are sixteen, teens are in the formal operational phase because they can learn to process more complex problems and more abstract thinking. At this stage, they understand the consequences of their deeds or misdeeds more clearly. However, sometimes teens grow a bit arrogant with their newfound mental abilities and a bit difficult to deal with because they may have diverse viewpoints, believing theirs is the most valid. Advanced mental development may be the result of dramatic brain growth during puberty and then a refining process seen in the late teen years.

Affective. The eight- to-ten-year-olds are advancing toward adolescence, and peer friendships start to become a high priority. They tend to cooperate in group settings and group games and dislike playing alone. They spend a lot of time talking with peers. They develop lasting friendships and begin to handle peer pressure. As they mature, they demonstrate growing independence, leading to concern with rules that can lead to bossiness. Teen pressure plays a big role in their behavior. Good and bad are defined by the teens' social standards. Social acceptance and individual identity are high priorities. They use problem-solving, negotiating, and compromising skills with their peers. They begin to develop sportsmanship and learn about winning and losing gracefully. They develop a high level of competence in competitive games and team sports. They become sensitive to what others think of them and seek adult approval. This is when clubs and groups become important. They can become critical of their own performance and begin to evaluate themselves. They express subtle emotions and experience moments of anger or frustration. With the hormones raging with some of the teens, they can be quite sensitive and overly dramatic; emotions can change quickly. Their self-esteem is extremely critical and can be fragile, which may lead to them being shy in public performances. This age group expects others to treat them as if they are fully-grown adults. They are very sensitive to criticisms. Encourage activities that provide group fun but not competition. Being team oriented, I always ask the group of teens to come up with a team name before the lesson starts. In the past, I got names, such as Snow Queens, Snow Kings, Pineapple Express, and the Seven Dwarves.

Physical. At this stage, there is an increase in body strength and manual dexterity. There is improved coordination and reaction time. There is an increase in large-muscle coordination, leading to success in organized sports and games. There is also an increase in small-muscle coordination, allowing them to learn complex craft skills; finger control is more refined. There is increased stamina. There is slow and steady growth with arms lengthening and hands growing. Periodic growth spurts can alter their coordination and athleticism, leading to awkwardness. As some parents will say, "It is unbelievable that it is so common for my son or daughter to stumble over a feather at this stage of development."

What Can You Expect as Realistic Goals for the 8- and older Age Group?

For the first lesson or two, considering the norm you can expect the following:

- Everything listed for the seven- to ten-year-old child.
- Ability to do linked-wedge C-turns down the entire beginner slope.
- Ability to manage bigger C-turns in a wedge at faster speeds.
- Ability to load, ride, unload the people mover conveyer belt safely.
- Ability to load, ride, unload the people mover or conveyer carpet and chairlift safely.
- Ability to maneuver their wedge turns around the cones (Set up as a race course), placed anywhere on the beginner hill.
- Ability to attempt shuffle turns, hop turns, and tap dance with the uphill/downhill ski.
- With subsequent lessons, Ability to do small bumps, rolling hills, hockey stops, parallel skiing.
- Ability to get up all four ways of getting up after falling (They may have a preference of their own).
- Know how to use different techniques to regulate their speed control

Coaching Tips. If you want a teaching challenge, try this group. Here are some tips to ensure success:

- They need to feel like a part of the group; do not single them out.
- Be their coach, friend, or mentor.

- With this age group it is easy to over-estimate their abilities and expectations. Always have realistic goals and not some idealistic goal that is not achievable or is unrealistic at the student's present performance level.[7,13]
- Be sensitive when providing feedback. Choose your words carefully. Be mindful that their self-esteem is very fragile with this age group.
- Let them have fun with their peers, but focus on the task.
- Keep your communication brief; they need to let off some steam after being in the classroom all day.
- No competitive drills or games; provide group activities.
- If they get emotional, talk to them as their mentor and treat them as an adult.
- If arrogance predominates with an individual, pull the child aside and provide alternative pathways to more acceptable behavior, like being the team leader, ski patroller, or assistant coach.
- If your students are shy and hesitate to participate, pair them up with their best friend.
- If they struggle to do a particular drill, be patient and help guide them through the difficult times.
- Kids at this age do not want to pretend. Reality is the name of the game. Do more realistic things that meets their peers' approval. Provide a basket full of positive comments and accolades for a job well done in front of all their peers.
- Never hesitate to ask for comments—good, bad, or ugly. They are all independent thinkers and have their own views about right and wrong.
- Be flexible with your teaching. Adapt to the situation. Aim to have fun and excitement with your drills.
- End your lesson with something that will be rewarding to everyone.
- Don't commit the cardinal sin by yelling or shouting at them in front of their peers. Voice matters. We may not be American singer, Harry Connick, Jr., with his soft, creamy, loving voice, but we can deliver with a more appealing tone.
- End on a happy note, and tell them how much you enjoyed skiing with them. I tell them," I hope to see you when I'm surfing! "

Bag of Tricks. What as a coach can you do for this particular age group of skiers? Here are some coaching tips that work:

- Small directional changes at first; then, more dynamic feats while remaining sticking within their limits (All three skills and balance).
- Picking one ski up as you traverse the hill (Balance).
- Falling leaf (All three skills and balance).
- Picking apples and putting them in the basket (Flexing and extending, pressure).
- Going into the terrain park (Fun and excitement).
- Game to see who can be the slowest down the hill by making the most turns (Fun and excitement, safety).
- Synchronized skiing for the more advanced groups (Fun and excitement, all three skills, and balance).
- Doing jumps with some air in the terrain park (Flexing and extending, pressure control, balance).
- Side slipping (Great drill for practicing edge control and balance).
- Carving (Fun; Five Fundamentals of Skiing[46]).
- Short-radius turns (Uses the Five Fundamentals of Skiing[46]).
- Getting down a small mogul field (All four skills).
- Simon says (Fun and excitement).
- Drawing contest in the snow (Fun and excitement).
- Pole touch (All three skills and balance; fun and excitement).
- Sing along; have them select a popular song (Fun and excitement).
- Going on narrow, undulating pathways through the trees (All three skills and balance; fun and excitement).
- Going on rolling hills (Waves), up and over and down the spine (Ridge) of a hill (All three skills and balance; fun and excitement).
- Having them pelt you with snowballs (Fun and entertainment).
- Opportunities for mileage: practice, practice, practice.

 Know how to coach all age groups. Based on the PSIA CAP Model. Understand the student's profile, and developmental limitations of each age group, formulate unique, fun-filled lessons tailored to fit the child's needs and expectations. Your goal is to get each child to perform to their maximum potential and to exceed their customer expectations.

CHAPTER 9

Developing a Strong Foundation—Coaching by the Zones

There is no universal system for categorizing skier ability levels. Ski resorts may have different classification systems. However, the basic method is beginner, intermediate, advanced, and expert. The PSIA American Teaching System uses the beginner zone, intermediate zone, and advanced zone. In this chapter, we will discuss only the highlights that should be covered for each performance zone.

Coaching the Beginner Performance Zone[2-6, 12-14, 16, 17, 32, 41, 46, 47, 52]

This group of skiers range from "never-ever" to those that can make wedge linked turns on a beginner hill (Green hill). The goal should be the knowing the fundamental movements to execute to improve wedge turns. The highlights of this lesson should be:

1. Introducing yourself to the parent and child.
2. Connecting and bonding with them.
3. Using the Skill Concept Model and Five Fundamentals of Skiing in their lessons.
4. Communicating to the parent your goals, where you will be coaching, what you will be coaching, how you will be coaching the movements and skills, and where you will meet them after the lesson. Get an agreement with the parent and child about your goals. See if it matches their goals.
5. Get the profile of the child by using the PSIA CAP Model[2-5, 13, 14,33,46,47,] Learning Partnership Model[16, 33, 46,] Learning Styles.[46]
6. Asking the child, "What do you want to do?" Be flexible.
7. Telling the child what you hope to accomplish during the lesson.
8. Coaching using the PADS[33] or STUMP Model.
9. Providing fun-loving adventures.
10. Following the Skiers' Motto (Safety, Fun, Learning).
11. Providing sufficient positive reinforcement.
12. Providing proper closure for both the parent and child.

13. Informing the parent and child, what the child's next lesson will be about.

Photo 47. A shy four-and-a-half-year-old girl with a big smile, which tells you she is very comfortable with her coach and has made good connections for very successful lessons.

Some key items to remember when coaching kids in the beginner zone:

- Checking the equipment. Are the bindings fitted properly? Are the skis the proper length (Tip height should be from the lower chin to nose)? For "never-ever" and relatively new skiers, the skis should be shorter (Chest height) for easier maneuverability. Have they put on their boots correctly and tightened the buckles sufficiently to ensure a snug fit?
- Are they dressed appropriately?
- Are their physiological needs met?[16, 31, 50]
- Do you have the tools necessary y for a safe and fun-filled lesson?
- Did you teach the athletic stance and checked it under different snow conditions, different terrains, and different maneuvers?
- When observing the gliding wedge run and strait run (Parallel skis), did you check where the COM is relative to the BOS?
- When teaching the wedge turn, is the student transferring weight to the new outside ski, and is the long leg promoting an edge angle?
- Did you check if the student is in proper alignment and has sufficient pressure to execute the turns by doing the glove-under-the-ski test?
- When performing the wedge turn, is the downhill ski flattening out due to the shorter leg; this allow gravity to pull the downhill ski tip away from the uphill ski tip?, Leg rotation of the downhill ski will accomplish the same thing; better yet, blend both mechanics during the turns.l

- While the inside ski is flatting, check whether to see the outside ski edge is engaging in the snow. Are the turns smooth and gradual, making a nice C-turn?
- Where is the COM? Is it primarily on the outside or inside ski during a turn?
- Is the body weight (Pressure control) on the outside or inside ski during a turn?
- Is the child linking their turns?
- What shape are the turns?
- Has speed control been extensively covered? (Did you review Figures 11, 13, and 17 thoroughly?)
- Have all the safety rules been covered? How did you check for validation of safety understanding?
- Small steps first. Start with small turns at the bottom of the hill; they will have to do side steps to climb the hill. If they are too little and struggle to climb you may want to push/pull them up the hill or pull them up with a plastic hoop or with your poles. Sometimes, you may simply want to take the skis off and carry them up the hill for them, then put them back on. I do this often to save time and to prevent the tiny tots from getting exhausted and to the point they can no longer do the drills. In photo 48, this four-year-old is working on her herringbone exercise (Duck walk with the ski tips pointing outward) on flat land before attempting to climbing the hill.

Photo 48. A shy four-year-old girl practicing her herringbone walk on flat land before attempting to climb the hill. To climb the hill, she will be encouraged to make a bigger ice-cream cone with her skis to create more edge angles for better traction.

- Has the child been taught ways to get up if the child falls?
- Do you know how to safely get the child on and off the conveyer belt or other transporting system? Do you know what to do if the child falls while riding up the people mover?
- If a kid is short (Butt below the chair), do you know how to safely pick up the child and ensure that the child does not slide off the chair? Is the child standing close to the chairlift operator, in case assistance is needed? Do you how to unload the child off the chair safely?
- Do you know what to do if there is a meltdown because of fear?
- Are you prepared for the special needs of a child (e.g., Autism, ADD, ADHD, diabetis, down's syndrome and food allergies)?
- Do you know what to do if your student in a serious accident?
- Do you have a Plan B or C if the weather conditions turn south (Blizzard, dropping temperature, high winds, rain)?
- Do you have the necessary materials in case your student has a runny nose, bloody nose, excessive tears due to the high winds, or any other conditions that needs caring attention? Keeping extra hand warmers in your pocket might be helpful
- What can you do if the skis have not been waxed for a long period of time and are sticking to the snow, resulting in difficulty turning? Keeping a small spray-on bottle or can of hand-rub wax in your pocket might be helpful.
- Do you have the telephone number of the front desk, hill supervisor, or ski patrol, and both their parents?
- How did you verify that your student comprehends the rules of safety?
- Do you have static homework for after class lessons to enhance their skills, particularly if there are deficiencies in their movements?
- Do you have a tactic to provide a lasting funny impression after closing your teaching lesson? For example, while holding the child's hand, we hop around like crazy bunnies, or I'll pull a hair wig out of my jacket and pretend I'm a character that the child really likes.

Photo 49. After a long afternoon skiing and lessons, the children and their coaches are still smiling because they enjoyed it so much.

Coaching the Intermediate Performance Zone[2,-5,7,12,14,16,17,33,34,41,46,47,52]

This group of skiers is more experienced and has more knowledge than the beginner zone group. The goal of this group should be focusing on getting the skier out of a wedge turn and beginning the parallel turns—first matching the skis before the fall line and then matching the skis after the fall line. It will take the blending of all of the skills to do it properly. The challenge will be linking the turns in a smooth, graceful, controlled manner. This open parallel turn should be your ultimate goal for this group of young turks. Don't fret if you observe skidding throughout the turns or even partial skidding at certain parts of the turns, such as during the apex of the turns. At their current skill level, it is to be expected when coaching this zone. The highlights of the lesson should be as follows:

1. You should cover everything discussed in the beginner zone. The movements you taught for wedge turns apply to the movements necessary for parallel turns.
2. This group of skiers can have their lesson first on the beginner terrain and then on the intermediate terrain (Blue hill).
3. For fun and entertainment, you can take them into the terrain park when they are more competent.

169

Key items to remember for coaching kids in the intermediate zone: [2-5, 7, 12, 13, 14, 16, 17, 33, 34, 41, 46, 47, 52]

- Cover everything discussed in the beginner zone.
- How do you instruct the progression of going from a wedge turn to a parallel turn? What is the sequence of events that must occur? What kind of terrain should you select when you start going from a wedge to a parallel turn?
- When is the weight transfer done and onto which ski? Is it the inside ski or outside ski? When transferring the COM, what phase of the turn should it take place? Which leg is extended and which leg gets shorter? Which foot has the predominant pressure (Heavy foot), and which foot has the lighter pressure (Light foot)?
- How do you instruct the matching of the skis before the fall line? After the fall line?
- What kind of drills and games can you employ to assist in the matching of the skis? Does pretending to be a stork, crane or flamingo; riding the scooter (Weight transfer to one ski); riding the bicycle (Long leg/short leg); hopping like a rabbit (Flexing and extending, pressure control); dancing by tapping the uphill ski on the snow while being balanced on the downhill ski; or pointing both headlights in the direction of the turn (Counter, balance) fit into your goal of turning skis and matching them?
- Can doing garlands[7] while traversing the hill help with the concept of weight transfer to one ski while twisting the leg of the other ski to match (Rotation)?
- Can a drill like doing side steps, playing the piano with the big toe and little toe, squashing the marshmallow with the inside and outside edges of the foot, and drawing smiley and sad faces in the snow with their boots assist with the concept of using edges for turning?
- Are you using rotary control as a blend with the other skills to assist in the turning process? Are you using the drill to make hourglass drawings with their boots or making a bow tie by pivoting the rotation on the arches of the feet to gain the concept of pointing your toes in the direction of the turn?
- Usually after they complete the turn, many skiers have their uphill ski ahead of the downhill ski. This causes the uphill hip to be ahead of the downhill hip, which can lead to a misalignment of the body which can cause imbalance. To fix that, one needs to have both ski tips even during the transition phase of the turn. If your COM is not over your BOS you can do one of two things; (1) flex your ankles more (Close), or (2) pull both feet back directly under your COM.

- How do you prevent them from looking down to see if they're doing pizza turns or French fry turns?
- Are you looking at their ski tracks in the snow to observe if they are in a wedge or parallel turn

Coaching the Advanced Performance Zone [2-5,8,12,17,20,24,29,33,34,39,41,46,47,52]

A major goal of this group is open parallel skiing and dynamic parallel skiing by learning how to carve.[21] Like all the other lesson plans for each zone, always find ways to introduce the static movement drills before you start the dynamic movement drills.

The second goal is to fine tune the blending the Skills Concept Model into the Five Fundamentals of Skiing.[46]

The third goal for this group is to refine their movements by making smoother transitions from turn to turn. I often tell my students, "Don't ski like robots; loosen up and make your movements more fluid." I will also tell them that I will crown them King/Queen of the Ice Cream Sundaes, and will pour hot fudge on the top of the sundae and for them to imagine its slowness and smoothness as it makes its way down. The point is don't let your advanced skier look stiff, instead add fluidity into skiing to look more graceful, effective, and efficient when making turns. The students should visualize and feel the smoothness of the child's skiing, which should be as smooth as hot butter flowing from one turn to the next.

Figure 19 A robot's movements are not fluid, but rather mechanical and jerky[46]

171

Photo 50. A pre-teen girl racing around the giant slalom gates by making carved turns at high speeds with good skiing fundamentals.[46]

The highlights of the lesson should be as follows:

1. Turning on corresponding ski edges.
2. Getting both skis away from the body.
3. Developing more edge angles.
4. Manipulating **DIRT** on command to make different shape and size turns.
5. Bending all skills while being in constant dynamic balance by following the Five Fundamentals of Skiing.[29]
6. Finishing the turns to control their speed by slowing down and by give time to regroup during the transition phases of the turns.
7. Knowing the different ways to control their speed.
8. Skiing on all terrains with varying degrees of steepness, including the advanced terrain (Black diamond).

Some of the key items to remember when coaching kids in the advanced zone[2-5, 8, 12-17, 33, 34, 39, 41, 46, 47, 52]

- Are they mentally, emotionally, and physically ready for this challenge?
- All of the things covered in the intermediate zone applies here.
- Do static drills, such as drawing smiley faces in the snow with the inside sole of the boot (Right and left); drawing sad faces in the snow with the outside edge

172

of the boot (Right and left); playing the piano with the big and pinky toes; or being a stork, crane, and flamingo help with teaching this segment of the lesson? Static drills should always precede dynamic drills.

- Do dynamic drills such as side slipping, pivot slips, falling leaf, and hockey stops assist with trying to achieve your goal for this zone?
- Most importantly, are they blending the Movement skills into the Five Fundamentals of Skiing.

Many techniques can help you establish your goals. Be mindful, like with other age groups and other performance zones, not all students can do these drills for whatever reason. As a coach, use proper judgements. For individuals who can do these advanced drills, you can try these maneuvers:

- Riding the bike: This drill emphasizes the importance of the long leg (Heavy foot) for increasing pressure and the shorter leg (Light foot) for decreasing pressure. You cannot have two long legs while riding the bike! The movements are a reciprocal action—one foot going down and the other going up with the other bike paddle. To look at this from a different angle: for one foot, the ankle is opening; for the other, the ankle is closing.
- Scooter turns: This activity promotes weight transfer to the outside ski and maintaining balance on predominately one ski. While balancing on one (Uphill or outside) scooter (Ski), try to maintain the balance while trying to turn by squashing the marshmallow and pointing the toes in the direction of the turn.
- Shuffle turns: This is a good exercise to check the child's alignment and balance. If your COM is behind the BOS the child will have difficulty in maintaining a smooth, continuous turn; you will see momentary pauses to regroup their athletic stance and, thus, balance, before they can continue shuffling nonstop throughout the turn.
- Outrigger turns: This drill emphases the need to get the legs as far away from the body to get more edge angle. As the child is traversing the hill and is balanced on the inside (Downhill) ski, extend the outside (Uphill) ski as far way from the body as possible, and apply ample pressure to start the turning process. Continue applying the correct amount of pressure throughout the turn do get the desired turn shape and size.

- Cowboy turns (Single-legged turns): This exercise stresses the importance of ankle articulation for change of directions. While balanced on one ski, try tipping the other ski from one side (Inside edge) and then to the other side (Outside edge).

- Two-legged turns: This is more difficult to do. The objective is to simultaneously have both skis tipped to the outside edge, and then both skis tipped to the inside edge.

- Upside-down turns: This exercise is another way of getting both skis away from the body at a great distance to achieve higher edge angles. This can be accomplished by not starting your next turn immediately down the hill. Instead, at the end of the turn, make an attempt to move the tips of your skis uphill and then dive through the door of the next turn. It is a scary process when you are that far away from both skis that are moving uphill and you're facing downhill to initiate your next turn!

- Dolphin turns: This is a great drill for extreme flexing and extending, for exerting pressure along the entire length of the skis, and the tips and tails of the skis. Start in a stationary athletic position and aggressively push your feet forward until your ski tips come off the ground; repeat as necessary until it is comfortably mastered. From a stationary athletic position, pull your heels up and your feet back (Retraction); repeat as necessary until is comfortably mastered. Now, combine both movements. Once there is enough pressure on the tail of the skis (So they are adequately bent), pull your feet back and your ski tips down. Make a traverse run on an easy terrain, while making these two movements dynamic, using a strong core. Still in traverse, join the two halves making a dolphin move. Practice until you can make actual dolphin turns. The turns are done after the skis are retracted and clear of the snow, landing on the other set of corresponding edges. In the beginning, look for little bumps to assist in these moves.

- Feeler turns: This activity emphasizes the need to articulate the ankles and knees to achieve edging while the body (Feet, ankles, knees, hip, shoulders and hands) are properly aligned to the slope of the hill as your student traverse the hill. To execute this, have the hands and poles extended with the baskets close to the ski tips and flexed enough to stay forward and be lower enough to allow ample ankle and knee movements side to side to make directional changes with the skis. Medium and large radius turns should be attainable.

- Double-fisted turns: This activity helps get both knees to move simultaneously the same amount in each direction. This can be both a static and dynamic drill. This exercise is especially important for girls and women. This gender is anatomically built differently from boys or men. For the female gender, it's a preparation for childbirth. In addition, girls are told by their mothers and grandmothers to always keep their knees together for proper etiquette. As a consequence, having the knees close together is a natural stance. In skiing we call it an A-frame, which compromises edging, pressure, rotary, and balance. With this drill, place the two fists between the knees and move the knees to the right and to the left. You can also do this exercise at home; you can also use a 4" rubber ball instead of the double fist to do this drill. Both knees should move in unison, simultaneously and to the same degree laterally! With very young kids, having them put each hand on each knee or on the femur of each leg may help with attaining parallel shins throughout the turns.

- Javelin turns: This drill is great for creating more counter, weight transfer to one ski, and more edge angle. To execute this drill, lift the inside ski and place the tip of the lifted ski on top of the tip of the outside ski, thus keeping the lifted ski at a slight angle to the ski on the snow. Balance on and turn exclusively on the inside edge of the outside ski, while tipping the lifted inside ski throughout the turn. The point of this drill is to work on and exaggerate the tipping of the inside foot, so tip from the ankle, allowing the knee to move/inside/forward a lot.

- Creating more upper body/lower body separation: This is a fundamental movement to create greater edge angles. To do this static exercise, have another person hold both pole baskets (One in each hand) as the student holds the handle to create a counter and extend both legs while letting the buttocks lower to the uphill ground. The lower the buttocks are to the ground; the more angulation will be created to obtain more edge angle.

- Pole Touch: Whether this lesson should be toward the end of the Intermediate Zone or this zone is a matter of debate. Pole touch, if taught correctly, has many uses: (1) it assists in fore/aft and lateral balance, (2) it assists in propelling the skier from point A to point B, (3) it acts as a timing device, (4) it stabilizes the upper body because of the three-point contact in the snow (Both legs and the pole), (5) it acts as a means of moving the inside shoulder toward the inside of the turn to help with extending the upper body forward to lead the turn. (6) it acts as a timing device to get a rhythm going when making linked turns. The proper body position are as follows: the arms and hands should be parallel to the ground, and the lower arms should spread open slightly to make the pole touch movements more efficient. The elbows are close to the rib cage and slightly forward. If the arms are straight ahead of you, the first movement is to move each arm laterally into the pole touch position, which is at the ten o'clock or eleven o'clock position on the clock when traversing the hill and one o'clock or two o'clock position on the other hand; this is a double movement. Ideally, the poles should be placed toward the ski tips and by making a "Y" in front of you, and not toward the binding. If you have the pole touch towards the binding, the shoulders will open up, throwing your upper body out of balance. There should be little arm movements during the planting of the poles; only wrist movements to get the basket to move forward and down into the snow. This is the signal that the skier should reach forward to turn around the pole; this movement allows the body to move into the turn and jeep him/her in dynamic balance. After making the turn, lift the pole basket out of the snow and slightly backward, toward the back. Picture a grandfather clock and the pendulum swinging back and forth, If the upper part of the clock and the pendulum swinging back and forth. If the upper part of the clock is not stable, the pendulum will lose control and swing irradicably. Thus, keep the upper torso stable at all times throughout the turns. Also, do not stab the salmon when you do the pole touch because it will delay the timing as you try to pull the tips out of the snow. This will cause your shoulders to open up and change the alignment of your body, throwing you off balance.

- Pivot Slip[40]: Great drill to learn to link turns in tight places. Mentally picture you doing a hockey stop in slow motion; it consists of doing a pivot and a slip by maneuvering the skis 180 degrees across the hill and sliding downhill within a narrow corridor. Start by keeping your shoulders and pole grip of the uphill pole facing downhill as you flatten your skis while side-slipping down the fall line;

this body position will create the necessary counter turn at the hip so that the skis can spring back to neutral when you make your 180 degrees turns. Do a deliberate pole placement to stabilize the upper body so you can use your legs freely to turn your skis. Secondly, extend the legs and center your weight over your feet as you point the ski tips into the fall line to flatten all four ski edges. Thirdly, quickly pivot your skis to point 180 degrees in the opposite direction. Flatten the skis to continue side-slipping down the fall line. Be sure to flex your legs to act as shock absorbers to absorb the irregularities in the snow. Keep your shoulders and hands forward and squarely facing downhill and ready for your next pole placement.

- Powder skiing[5, 42]: Can be a lot of surprising fun. Coaching powder skiing is an art and is technically different from alpine skiing. First, you need to get the appropriate skis; wider skis (Greater than 100 mm at the waist) and with a large front rocker. The powder technique requires being relaxed and balanced on both feet with both the ski tips pointing slightly upward (By flexing at the ankles and knees). The skis are closer together than regular alpine skiing to move both skis simultaneously together and in unison as you change direction in a hopping movement (Flexing and extension). At the top of the hop (Extension), point the skis in the new direction (Rotational control) as the upper torso faces downhill.

Photo 51. This lucky, young fella is experiencing total bliss because he is not only weaving through a ton of trees, but also through deep, fluffy powder.

There are many other things that you can coach in this zone if the child is prepared:

- Moguls
- Racing
- Freestyle
- Steeper terrain (Double and triple-black diamond)
- Synchronized skiing
- Skiing through trees
- Jumping off of cornices
- Back Bowls
- Skiing backwards
- 360 maneuvers on snow

I would like to briefly mention a few things about Racing. The kids in the intermediate and advanced zones seem to love learning the mechanic of racing. In all of my twenty years of coaching, racing ranks on the top of children's excitement and choice of things to do, followed by doing freestyle activities in the Terrain Parks. Once the racing gates are set up, I undoubtedly get undivided attention of every student. So, as a coach, you may want to learn the ABCs of racing and give it a shot. Racing will help enforce the use of the Five Fundamentals of Skiing. If you have not had the opportunity to take your student into the terrain park you may not want to continue onto the road less traveled. You may wish to take freestyle clinics and take the higher road to having your students have fun in the terrain Parks.

Photo 52. A teenage girl using the Five Fundamentals of Skiing Model to make carved turns around the racing gates.

As a final reminder on children's safety because it is so important, as the performance level increases, as the difficulty of the drills become more complex, as the steepness of the terrain become more challenging, and as the speed increases, the danger also increases. The last thing that you want as a coach is to have to report to the parents their child has been in a nasty accident (See figure 20).

Figure. 20 A child has been in a nasty accident

In addition, with the pandemic surrounding us, practice safety at all times (See photo 53).

Photo 53. During the COVID-19 pandemic, many new safety rules have been implemented at the ski resorts. Here you have a seven-year-old boy (Wearing a mask) taking a private lesson from his coach (Wearing a double face mask).

When an outstanding coach teaches his students well you will have an outcome seen in photo 54.

Photo 54. Mom and her 12-year-old daughter are jubilant because of the bonding and trust that they developed with the coach; In addition, they are thrilled with the rapid learning curve that their daughter made to be an advanced skier— whereby she has set her goal to be a ski instructor when she is of age.

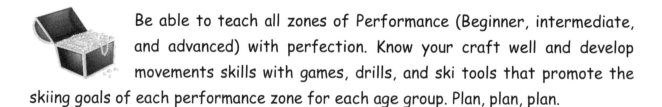

Be able to teach all zones of Performance (Beginner, intermediate, and advanced) with perfection. Know your craft well and develop movements skills with games, drills, and ski tools that promote the skiing goals of each performance zone for each age group. Plan, plan, plan.

CHAPTER 10
Closing Thoughts

In closing, I would like to leave you with some motivational thoughts. The ingredients for success are studying your trade intently, practice to perfection, and teach with a passion.

Bo Eason[18], an All-Pro NFL safety, once said, "Be the best in the world at what you do; there's no plan B for you're a game." As a coach for kids, develop the characteristics of being a Champion and a Leader. Develop a voracious appetite and deep passion for Learning. The important thing is to also be mindful that your attitude and understanding contribute greatly to the success of your students. With your guidance and support, these kids can develop not only skiing skills, but life skills such as self-confidence, decision-making abilities, and ability to solve problems with a moral compass that always points to True North.

Remember, to keep the parents involved because we have an awesome responsibility and opportunity to impact their lives. We are not just teaching skiing; we are teaching special people to ski, the future of our ski industry! Study your trade with intensity, practice to perfection, and teach with a passion. In addition, solve challenges with a moral compass that always point to True North.

There are three major pillars that you must always keep in mindful awareness as a great coach:

I.   People Skills Fundamentals[46]

- Develop relationships built on trust.
- Engage in meaningful two-way communication.
- Identify, understand, and manage your emotions and actions.
- Recognize and influence the behaviors, motivations, and emotions of others.

II.   Teaching Skills Fundamentals[46]

- Collaborate on long-term goals and short-term objectives.
- Manage information, activities, terrain selection, and pacing.
- Promote play, experimentation, and exploration.
- Facilitate the learner's ability to reflect upon experiences and sensations.
- Adapt to the changing needs of the learner.
- Manage emotional and physical risks.

III. Alpine Skiing Fundamentals[46]

- Control the relationship of the COM to the BOS to direct pressure along the length of the skis.
- Control pressure from ski to ski and direct pressure toward the outside ski.
- Control edge angles through a combination of inclination and angulation.
- Control the ski rotation (Turning, pivoting, steering) with leg rotation, separate from the upper body.
- Regulate the magnitude of pressure created through ski/snow interaction.

WELCOME TO THE MAGICAL WORLD OF SKIING!

 I have an idea_e and a dream to be able to influence every ski instructor, coach, and teacher to be inspired to achieve greatness by allowing the child's maximum energy to fulfill children's desires and dreams.

Photo 55. Little boy exuberant because he made it to the top—he felt that he was on top of the world.

_e_ . Used with permission from Microsoft

REFERENCES

This manual would not be possible without the input from our skilled and experienced reviewers and from the multiple resources that have already been published:

1. Adaptive Snowsports Instruction; PSIA Education Foundation, Lakewood, Colorado, 2003; 108 pages.

2. Adult Alpine Teaching Handbook; PSIA; Vail and Beaver Creek Ski & Snowboard Schools; Beaver Creek, Colorado, 2011; 318 pages.

3. Alpine Handbook; PSIA Educational Foundation; Lakewood, Colorado,1996; 77 pages.

4. Alpine & Snowboard Teaching Handbook; Vail Resorts Management Co.; Vail, Colorado; 2004; 200 pages.

5. Alpine Technical Manual; PSIA; PSIA/AASI American Snowsports Education Foundation, Inc.; 2014; 150 pages.

6. Alpine Level I Study Guide; PSIA; PSIA Educational Foundation; Lakewood, Colorado, 1996; 126 pages.

7. Alpine Level II Study Guide; PSIA; PSIA Educational Foundation, Lakewood, Colorado, 1996; 95 pages.

8. Alpine Level III Study Guide; PSIA; PSIA Educational Foundation, Lakewood, Colorado, 1996; 111 pages.

9. Anderson, John; "Captain Zembo's Ski & Snowboarding Teaching Guide for Kids."; PSIA Education Foundation; Lakewood, Colorado, 2nd ed., 1996; 33 pages.

10. Campbell, Stu, Lundberg, Max, and PSIA; "The Way to Ski: The Official Method"; The Body Press; Los Angeles, California, 1986; 159 pages.

11. Chapman, Gary; "5 Love Languages"; Northfield Publishing; 2nd Ed.; Plano, Texas; 2015; 203 pages.

12. Children's Alpine Teaching Handbook; PSIA/AASI Intermountain (Northwest); American Snowsports Education Association, 2010; 314 pages.

13. Children's Instruction Manual; PSIA Education Foundation; 1997; 151 pages.

14. Children's Instruction Manual, 2nd Ed.; PSIA Education Foundation; Lakewood, Colorado, 2008; 128 pages.

15. Clelland, Mike; "Ski Tips for Kids: fun instructional techniques with cartoons!"; Falcon Guides; Guilford, Connecticut, 2013; 103 pages.

16. Core Concepts for Snowsports Instructors: Teaching; PSIA/AASI Education Foundation; Lakewood, Colorado, 2008; 90 pages.

17. Cues to Ineffective and Effective Teaching; American Snowsports Education Foundation; PSIA, Educational Foundation, Lakewood, Colorado, 2008; 12 pages.

18. Eason, Bo; There's No Plan B for You're a-Game; St. Martin's Press, New York, New York, 2019;258 pages.

19. Elbee, Viviane; "Teach your Giraffe to Ski"; Albert Whitman & Co.; Park Ridge, Illinois, 2018; 32 pages.

20. Elling, R. Mark; "The All-Mountain Skier: The Way to Expert Skiing"; Ragged Mountain Press; New York, New York, 2004; 240 pages.

21. Fellows, Chris; "Tactics for All-Mountain Skiing"; PSIA Education Foundation, Lakewood, Colorado, 2006; 108 pages.

22. Hamilton Ray J.; "Squirrels on Skis"; Random House Books; New York, New York, 2013; 64 pages.

23. Harb, Harold; "Harald Herb's Essentials of Skiing'; Hatherleigh Press; Long Island City, New York, 2010; 203 pages.

24. Heckelman, Martin; "The New Guide to Skiing"; W. W. Norton & Company; New York, New York, 2001; 144 pages.

25. Herrin, Nicholas; "PSIA-AASI's Commitment to Snowsports Education: Is outlined in Best Practices for Teaching During COVIID-19"; 32 Degrees; American Snowsports Education Foundation; Lakewood, Colorado, Fall 2020; pages 45-47.

26. Jay, Joshua; "Magic: The Complete Course; Workman Publishing Company; New York, New York, 2008; 288. Pages.

27. Kazanjian, Kirk; Exceeding Customer Expectation; Random House Publishing; New York, New York, 2007; 256 pages.

28. Kolb, Alice and Kolb, David; Eight Important Things to Know About the Experimental Learning Cycle"; Australian Educational Leader (40), Issue 3, 2018.

29. LeMaster, Ron;" Ultimate Skiing"; Human Kinetics Publishers, Inc; Champaign, Illinois, 2009; 224 pages.

30. Ludlow, Libby; "A-B-Skis: An Alphabet Book About the Magical World of Skiing"; Kickstarter Publishing, 2019; 32 pages.

31. Maslow, A.; "A Theory of Human Motivation'; Psychological Review 50:370-396 (1943)

32. Munsterer, Rebecca; The Little Rippers; Novel Nibble Publishing; Norwich, Vermont; 2013

33. New Snowsports Instructor Guide; PSIA/AASI Intermountain (West); PSIA Education Foundation; Lakewood, Colorado, Colorado, 2018; 27 pages.

34. Park and Pipe Instructor's Guide: Freestyle; PSIA/AASI American Snowsports Education Foundation, 2005; 156 pages.

35. Pavia, Audrey; "Horses for Dummies"; John Wiley & Sons; Columbus Publishing Labs; Zainesville, Ohio,1999; 400 pages.

36. Penske, Ned; "The Pursuit of Happiness"; PSIA-C Central Line; PSIA/AASI Frankfort, Michigan, 2017; Issue 4; F6-7 pages.

37. Phipps, Stephen and Liedtke, Judy; "Weekend Warriors Guide to Expert Skiing"; DaoEn Corporation; Boise, Idaho, 2008; 224 pages.

38. Pogue, David; "Magic for Dummies"; IDG Books Worldwide, Inc; New York, New York, 1998; 369 pages.

39. Roberts, Delia; An Instructor's Guide to a Healthy Immune System: How to Improve Your Resistance to Diseases, Including COVID-19; 32 Degrees; American Snowsports Education Association; Lakewood, Colorado; Winter 2021; Pages 76-80, 94-98.

40. Rogan, Michael; Essential Skill: The Pivot Slip; Ski Magazine; Boulder, Colorado; November 2020; page 46-47.

41. Rueda, Claudia; "Bunny Slopes"; Chronicle Books; Columbus, Ohio, 2016; 60 pages.

42. Schorling, Ann; Powder Play: Four Tips to Maximize Float and Fun in Powder; Ski Magazine; Boone, Iowa; Page 44-45.

43. Snowboard Teaching Handbook; Product number 121PSIA Education Foundation; Lakewood, Colorado, 2015; 358 pages.

44. Stadelman, Paul and Fife, Bruce; "Ventriloquism Made Easy"; Piccadilly Books, Ltd.; Colorado Springs, Colorado, 2003; 108 pages.

45. Swift, Sally; "Centered Riding"; St. Martin's Press; New York, New York, 1985; 208 pages.

46. Teaching Snowsports Manual; American Snowsports Education Association, Inc. Lakewood, Colorado, 1918; 262 pages.

47. Vail and Beaver Creek Children's Alpine Teaching Handbook; Vail Resorts Management Co.; Vail Colorado, 2004; 200 pages.

48. Valar, Paul and Johnston, Jimmy; "Skiing"; The Athletic Institute; Sterling Publishing Co., New York, New York, 1966; 93 pages.

49. Van Dusen, Chris; "Learning to Ski with Mr. Magee"; Columbus Publishing Labs; Zanesville, OH 2010; 36 pages.

50. Wahba, A., and Bridgewell, L. "Maslow Reconsidered: A Review of Research on the Need of Hierarchy Theory; Organizational Research and Human Performance; 15: 212-240 (1976).

51. Weston, Hannah and Bedingfield, Rachel; "Connecting Training: The Heart and Science of Positive Horse Training"; Connection Training Ltd.; Elsevier Publishing, 2019; 634 pages.

52. 2020 Ski Instructor Survival Guide; Deer Valley Ski Resort; Deer Valley, Utah, 2019; 206 pages.

53. 2020 ADA Standards of Medical Care in Diabetes; American Medical Association, Muncie, Indiana, 2019; 206 pages.

Lightning Source UK Ltd.
Milton Keynes UK
UKHW020414160223
417035UK00015B/251